The Sales Focused CEO

Looking at Business Through a New Lens

Author: Adele Crane

ISBN: 1522829695
ISBN 13: 9781522829690

Distributed by: CreateSpace, LLC, an Amazon.com company

Cover design by Sales Focus International, United States

Other Books and Publications by the Author:

2001 – *Get Sales Focused: Rethinking and Revolutionizing Sales Forces and Sales Results*

2009 – *Building the Most Effective Sales Force in the World: the Era Post the Global Financial Crisis.*

About the Author

Adele Crane is a leading and highly respected international business consultant with more than twenty-five years of experience working in Australia, New Zealand, the United Kingdom, South Africa, and various parts of Asia and North America. Managers throughout the world rely on her expertise in leading change and growth, and she is widely considered to be a thought leader.

Adele's consultancy work—through cultural change, sales transformations, and the development of high-performance teams—has produced results for hundreds of organizations in many different industries. She is arguably one of the most experienced experts in this field in the world today. Major media forums across the world have recognized her success. She has shared the stage with some of the most recognized and successful CEOs and business thought leaders during the course of her career.

Adele has conducted more than two hundred in-depth business reviews and has developed plans that have assisted companies in achieving tens of millions of dollars of top-line revenue and above-industry-standard profits. Her sales leadership capability has been demonstrated many times over. She has personally delivered profitable revenue improvements across many industries in 90 to 120 days—with sustainable growth achievements in excess of 40 percent in each company serviced—and she has delivered more successful turnarounds in the past decade than any other known consultant.

Adele is renowned for her extraordinary diagnostics of businesses and her ability to provide candid and in-depth knowledge that assists companies in realizing their revenue improvement. Senior executives seek Adele's analytical capabilities when they aim to transform their sales organizations by establishing the right priorities for their projects; such executives value her keen eye for both top-line and bottom-line profitability.

Adele's depth of knowledge and expertise in sales organizations has made her one of the world's foremost authorities in this field.

Introduction

Companies fear looking at changes or improvements to their sales forces for good reason: sales is the engine that drives revenue. No matter how patched up or sputtering that engine may be, the thought of overhauling it fills CEOs and senior executives with dread. To keep revenue flowing, companies will make ongoing, piecemeal repairs as long as they can. They will tolerate behavior and performance that would not be tolerated in any other areas of the business.

At a certain point in time in the life cycle of any company, changes or improvements need to be made to the sales and marketing area of a business. The world is not static, and sales and marketing organizations cannot be allowed to stagnate and operate in their now-primitive business processes. The sales business, in particular, has become the last frontier for people to address in business improvement. Fear of the unknown, and the use of the wrong lens to view the business, are the greatest barriers to overcome.

CEOs have traditionally relied on being presented with reports of financial information on organizational performance. Each report demonstrates performance against the previous year and the year-to-date to allow for making comparisons and seeing whether improvements have been achieved. These CEOs are flying blind, since they attempt to relate the financial report to the strategy they've set in place for the company.

Financial information about real sales organization performance can be dangerously misleading. When a company is experiencing a drop in sales, traditional financial statements can understate the seriousness of the situation. Having a strategy that is more sophisticated than merely relying on financial reports can allow your company to steer clear before any indicators appear that there is trouble ahead. In fact, according to research by strategist Dan Prosser, only 13 percent of companies deliver strategy.

The first step for any CEO is to be empowered with knowledge of how the sales and marketing business should function, and dispose of any of the myths and legacies that work in opposition to delivering that strategy. Most information that people expose themselves to is written by sales leaders for sales leaders. It is narrow in content and focuses on compensation plans, training, and ingenuous reporting; all support the mystique of the sales business. Marketing cannot become a more open and transparent area of the business until reporting in a meaningful manner is a requirement.

This book is written by a CEO for CEOs, and is based on more than twenty-five years of consulting with CEOs in business turnarounds and improvement. It looks at the broader demands of business that you as a CEO must deal with; it establishes the thinking you require and the new lens you need to view the sales and marketing business. In short, it assists you in becoming what I refer to as a sales focused CEO.

Sales focused CEOs delve deeper into critical detail, driving growth and removing any barriers that stop strategy execution. They embrace business improvement and may gain value from "lean" principles in their businesses. As CEOs, they rely less on the sales leaders' verbal representations and traditional reporting and place more emphasis on fact-based information, which provides a rich and steady view of both the present and the future.

They do not follow the "grand theory of everything" that you read about in business journals; they have learned that the detail is critical, and they apply different drivers for their business that will ensure that strategy execution is achieved.

Sales are the "make and break" for most companies, and comes with high risk. When performing well, sales remains the untouched frontier. When things go wrong, however—usually for a sustained period of time—it becomes necessary to take action. The person in charge of managing one of the highest risks for most companies is an underperforming sales leader—one who is frequently an immovable person who has wrapped him- or herself in mystique and has a connection with the most important element of business: the customer. Only when armed with the knowledge and confidence of how this business unit should operate does anyone take steps to address these shortcomings. In order to mitigate risks, sales focused CEOs embrace business processes and disciplines that will give them immediate transparency deep inside the business.

Through the process of improvement, the sales focused CEO views sales and marketing like any other area of the company. Lean principles transcend into sales and marketing business when applied correctly. This is not a matter of the sales process, but rather the business of sales and the business of marketing. The principles that are applied free up capacity, thus removing excessive operating costs associated with sales, reducing fixed costs, and providing the ability to maximize profit. The productivity of the sales and marketing organization becomes focused, streamlined, and effective.

These processes have been honed over many years through different industries and business challenges. They challenge the thinking of the masses as they follow the usual commercial route.

This book will potentially challenge the thinking of a CEO, create a new view of how sales and marketing organizations should operate and, most important, provide an understanding of how other companies have achieved growth of 25 to 40 percent year-on-year in developed companies. Those companies that do manage this deliver 50 to 80 percent more profit in their businesses than their competitors; these are the 13 percent of enterprises that do deliver strategy.

The Sales Focused CEO creates a new lens for looking at fresh business thinking for the contemporary world in which we operate.

Table of Contents

With the new lens, you will have greater insights into the sales business, thus providing you with a platform for improved decision making at all levels within the sales and marketing business. The alignment of the units creates a force in how the company goes to market and delivers strategy in a timely and cost-effective manner. The sales focused CEO works with new goals and targets, a new culture, and fresh thinking about ways to maximize the performance of this critical business unit.

As you can imagine, people must change with any initiatives and changes. As CEO, you must be comfortable with making other people uncomfortable if you hope to achieve results. You need to change the business philosophy to its core to achieve the change that will deliver the results you want. If these wholesale changes are not made, your business will face challenges in reaching its full capability.

Many sales leaders are at best only capable of continuing the natural flow of the business, based on the momentum that is created through the product and brand. They deliver very few initiatives that will have a lasting and positive effect on a business. When the brand/product begins to exhaust itself, they quickly become the custodians of a failing sales organization. They will make traditional, low-impact attempts to improve results, but they will not make sufficient changes to the trajectory that the business is now on. Their impact of non-performance reaches deep into the organization.

Many of the strategic plans are sound and make good commercial sense. What I also see is that companies often attempt to deliver these plans several years in a row but simply cannot seem to get them off the ground. The bottom line is that many companies simply don't know how to implement the strategy, whether it is within sales, marketing, or other areas of the business.

Writing sales strategy is a matter of business excellence. High-performance sales organizations do not just happen by chance. They are the result of careful planning, as well as hiring the right people who will align strategy and the marketplace to deliver the required results.

Because many CEOs miss the early warning signs of looming problems, they often deal with issues that have gained traction and need more time and effort to remedy. Sales and marketing are filled with early warning signs to which you need to respond.

Reducing costs is often associated with a poorly operating company in need of finding profits—quickly. Successful companies know that cost reduction is an ongoing process and one that requires vigilance at all times. Such companies consider cost reduction to be more like waste reduction. The diligent sales focused CEO will continually look at these points of waste elimination within the sales and marketing businesses, and will constantly assess them for improvements.

The talent in any organization defines its success. Talented people in marketing and sales have a very high profile and obvious capability, both to the customers and within the company. The sales focused CEO like you sets the bar high when hiring for these two areas and demands evidence of their talents through their delivery of your strategy. The pitfalls of hires are set out within.

Many companies have been indoctrinated into believing that the sales force measurements that should be applied include financial reports with gross margins and pipeline reports. These are insufficient to gain full transparency of the sales force and drive improvement. The right reporting and purpose is explained.

Sales forces are renowned for poor or no reporting. This relentless chase often sees sales leaders give up and resort to making phone calls in order to acquire updates about the latest news, hoping to generate less paperwork while doing so than they would while generating reports. There is a new game and the sales forces are playing it.

Sales operations people are forms of analytical sales managers. They bring the sales focused CEO rich information in clean reporting formats in order to support high-quality decision making and reduce the risk of wandering off strategy. They ensure that the sales business works according to a well-defined sales strategy implementation process.

Chapter 22:
Removing the Chasm between Marketing and Sales

Undoubtedly for many companies, although they may have strategies in place, they do not have sales plans in place; that situation dislocates the marketing organization's ability to define the actions that are required to generate sufficient leads to support the sales organization's activities. The lack of planning also inhibits the ability to produce leads within defined markets that will support strategy.

Chapter 23:
Bringing It All Together

The sales focused CEO is the person who is most capable of delivering greater revenue, profits, and value to the business. When you as CEO are focused on marketing sales, you will create a highly competitive company that is capable of growth—well above your counterparts in other companies.

01 The Untold Truth about Product-Driven Organizations

You are a successful chief executive officer (CEO) or managing director who leads a company that has enjoyed growth and profit and has developed a strong brand in the market. Each year you communicate your strategy for continued growth—sometimes achieving it, other times not. The profitability fluctuates, and some years require you to tighten the company belt, while others are more generous. The balance sheet looks good, and the company has become a valuable asset to its shareholders, whether public or private. The company has a loyal customer base, which provides a degree of predictable income in the years ahead.

You look at competitors, other well-known brands in the same market, and they are gaining market share, expanding, and seemingly delivering greater profits. You naturally investigate what they're doing that is delivering greater organic growth than your company. If you take a step back, the history of your company will most likely show the development of a great product (or the acquisition of the rights to sell a great product). The company then hired people who had a passion for the product and who could share a great vision for assisting people in becoming customers who would use the product.

The people in your company are passionate; and technical/product knowledge and industry experience have become the core of all hiring decisions.

Those people who have the added quality of having strong connections are rising quickly in the business—whether in operations, finance, or any other function within the company. There is a sense of comfort in having these people on the team, because they "get it."

Marketing has been active through various channels, building the brand and awareness of the company and its products and services. You have developed unique propositions that you take to the market, thus allowing customers to make informed decisions about purchasing your offerings over those of other companies.

The company takes significant modernization steps to increase the profitability of the business, and it improves financial controls as a way to reduce operational costs, increase operational efficiencies, and improve the quality of the products. Some companies have embarked on the lean methodology journey, while others have adopted other principles that directly contribute to improvements.

Typically, the next step is to focus on people: your greatest asset. During this stage, the company develops people's leadership skills and their capability to contribute to strategic planning. The company has a worthy vision, a great product, and excellent people, and it is operationally effective.

Your competitors are doing the same thing. What they learned is taught in business schools throughout the world and comes from advisors who were graduates of similar business schools. The questions now are: How do you go beyond your competitors? What is the next step you should take to set you apart from your competitors? How do you as CEO build that next level that will take the company from great to exceptional? How do you increase your personal value as a CEO?

The challenge for most CEOs is that most are following the same path, the same process that all other CEOs are walking, with the same thinking and processes that bring you to the same place in time. The CEO who delivers beyond the others is the one who takes on fresh thinking, stepping onto a new path that will take him or her on a journey that uses contemporary practices. These are not high-level concepts from business journals, nor are they processes that have been developed by people who have never been in the trenches—those who have not grown businesses, but rather, have benefited from the momentum generated by large corporations that roll on despite poor decision making, poor management, and major changes in the market.

The CEO who will be of value in the future is that person who can deliver greater profits than others in a comparable industry—one who understands that the top line matters as much as the bottom line and manages both effectively, and one who creates a valuable asset for privately owned companies, or significant value for shareholders in public companies. These CEOs do not just apply a method that everyone else follows. They adopt a way of thinking that is fundamentally different from that which is taught in business schools. They make difficult decisions and go the extra mile that will take them to the realm of being great leaders and CEOs.

02 Your Strategy Is Derailed

I recently delivered a presentation at a conference in New Zealand to approximately two hundred CEOs in which I discussed strategy execution. The general content of the strategies the participants used included offshore expansion and new products to market; since their market was a smaller population, this was not uncommon. I asked for a show of hands of those CEOs who'd had their strategies delivered in a timely manner over the previous twenty-four months and who had achieved their revenue forecasts. Roughly fifteen people raised their hands, some a little nervously or reservedly. I then asked who of those had sales forces that were responsible for delivery, and most put their hands down.

I next asked which companies had full-time sales forces, and about half to two-thirds of the people in the room raised their hands. The next question started to sort the performance of those sales forces. "Those who delivered 5 to 10 percent under forecast revenue, please put your hands down." There was a noticeable reduction in the numbers. "Those who delivered less than 70 percent of forecast revenue, please put your hands down." A few more hands dropped. This left a group of people who delivered in the range of 75 to 90 percent of forecast revenue. I asked the group to keep their hands up if their sales leaders were still employed by them. All but three or four people kept their hands up.

This anecdotal research indicated that most companies accept underperformance in the most obvious area of revenue attainment. Underperformance is a direct failure to deliver a part of the company strategy and has repercussions across many areas of the business, as strategic planning is not just about revenue. It is used to set priorities, focus energy and resources, strengthen operations and finance, and ensure that employees and other stakeholders are working toward common goals. The strategy sets the organization's direction in response to changing environments. In the context of this book, all of those elements require funding that is primarily drawn from the revenue attained by the sales force.

The dilemma that every CEO faces at some stage of his or her career is that sales forces are not delivering forecast numbers. Some face this dilemma on a year-on-year basis, while some have fluctuating exposure to the problem. As CEO, your company's strategy each year forms part of a three- or five-year plan, and each year that strategy is not achieved, you must adjust or redefine it. At the start of the financial year, you experience a sense of urgency for revenue performance to be attained, as it directly affects your cash flow and sets the momentum for the coming periods. If you have not reached your goals in the previous years, you face even more pressure. Other areas of the business are reliant on the company achieving those numbers in order to afford many of the other elements of the strategy related to operations, finance, and employee headcounts and talent.

You are fully aware that the culture of the business suffers when sales are not kicking the numbers over the line each month, quarter, and year, but it seems that most companies accept this situation as "normal." They prefer to manage the risk than to manage the sales leaders.

In the first quarter of any financial year, there is always a sense of optimism that this year will be different.

As you move into the second quarter, however, you start to question how your sales business is operating. If you are trending below your anticipated targets, you may start to ask questions of your sales leader:

- Why aren't we hitting our goals?

- Are we all on the same page with what is required?

- Why can't our people execute?

These are seemingly simple questions that all too often have complex answers that cannot be fixed easily. You need to look for the symptoms rather than listen to your sales leader's answers. The sales leader will present you with a deflection if he or she has any inclination of the potential issues you have.

Some obvious symptoms can lead you toward discovering what the problems are, but without the right investigation you may be going on a wild-goose chase. You need to be aware of the symptoms before you can start working on the actual causes and making the necessary changes.

The symptoms set out below directly correlate to poor strategic traction and manifest in three common behavioral indicators that your leaders may be presenting to you.

1. Complacency Symptom
The company has been performing well, achieving (or nearly achieving) its goals. It has not taken any drastic action for short delivery of goals by, say, 5 percent or 10 percent, and has accepted the seemingly plausible reasons for these shortcomings. The sales leader believes the business has sufficient momentum to keep going, based on his or her experience in the industry. The top ten, twenty, or thirty customers are buying, and all seems to be going fine. The sales figures show a few wins, indicating the potential for the company to attain revenue.

The marketing organization has delivered some good campaigns, and they are optimistic. There is a sense in the company that everyone is connected to the market and knows what's going on. The market feedback you get from the salespeople is that the company is in a good position.

These false perceptions, which are supported by the general sense of activity in the business, do not provide a catalyst for alarm. The sales business believes that it is rolling along in the desired direction.

The problem is that there is no risk strategy in place for addressing market changes, or that competitive shifts and complacency are making your company operate in neutral. The company's natural momentum is keeping it gliding in the market, and the feedback you get comes from existing customers, where the reports will most likely be positive. These reports may be insufficient for identifying subtle changes in the market, and the market may be slowly pulling the company farther away from its profitable path. Only after several months will the company realize that the market has shifted, and then it will need to take action to find that market again. Unfortunately, given the complacency syndrome, it can sometimes take a sales leader nine to twelve months to take action. The degree of action he or she takes is not sufficient to bring the company back on track, which means that your strategy is being derailed.

2. Confusion Syndrome
Your company's strategy is clear, and you have discussed it at length with the team leaders. Both marketing and sales have agreed that they understand what is required of them, but was that understanding transmitted properly to the teams that report to them? How did the team leaders convey that information? Have they communicated all the necessary information to their respective teams?

If they have not communicated that information effectively, then you need to ask yourself: Did they understand it?

Can they articulate the strategy back to you with sufficient detail that will instill confidence? Have you reviewed their communication strategy for information dissemination? Sales and marketing leaders often delay implementation due to a lack of understanding, which may be compounded by the fear of seeking more information in an effort to save face and protect their reputations.

3. Priority

So many sales and marketing leaders battle competing priorities: when you are up to your ears in day-to-day demands and crises, it's hard to remember that your primary directive is to implement the strategy. Many sales and marketing leaders find it challenging to make the transition from working in the business to working on the business. They feel their best contribution will be working within the team, rather than guiding the team. They have lost the focus on strategy implementation and on ensuring that the team is being guided on the right course at all times. Leaders must not allow the business to pull them in directions that may be in opposition to the plan.

If you identify with any of these symptoms in your company, then you should be hearing alarm bells. It is important for you to understand the common issues other CEOs confront and to recognize most sales leaders' patterns of behavior. This will contribute to your thinking and decision-making prowess.

03 Research Has Alarm Bells Ringing

The research that follows is a few years old, but it will be relevant for many years because the industry of sales management changes at a glacial pace. The research paper I discuss in this chapter has been pivotal in assisting companies in gaining improved outcomes with their sales organizations or sales business units.

In 2012, my company, Sales Focus International (SFI), conducted extensive research and case studies of 480 companies to answer the question, "Are you better positioned to excel in 2013 and beyond?" This report offers CEOs valuable insights for assisting them in their sales organizations' preparedness, and their ability to deliver strategy and forecast revenue.

The focus of the research and studies is a combination of both the CEOs' perspective toward the sales organization and the sales leaders' perspective toward their organizational performance. This study also provided valuable insights into the effect that sales leaders have on the company, both within the sales organization and on the broader audience across the company.

Looking at the previous four years from the time of the report, the research demonstrated that 88 percent of CEOs had been compelled to take action to manage costs and efficiencies within the actual sales organization. Within that group, 71 percent reported that they had been forced to take more than one action in response to changing economies and markets.

CEOs reported that they'd given directives to sales leaders to reduce costs in the following areas:

- Compensation plans   64 percent
- Hiring   76 percent
- Travel/entertainment   54 percent
- Headcount   41 percent
- Goals and quotas   26 percent
- Sales operating expenses   37 percent
- Sales cost   29 percent
- Training and development   12 percent

These cuts went deep into the sales organizations and how they operated, which tended to downsize the sales business overall. The noticeable trend was that the cuts were mainly in hiring and compensation plans, since these are the primary cost points. Interestingly, only a small number of respondents reported reductions in training and development, and that was driven by the fact that no expense budget was in place from the outset in these cases.

The CEOs were pleased to report that these overall reductions had shown immediate benefits with respect to cash flow and profitability. Their primary concern—and an overriding issue—was that most respondents reported that they experienced challenges in the delivery of sales goals and quotas (that is, their budgets), even after making reductions.

In identifying the instigator of these changes, more than 95 percent of the CEOs were driven by the financial manager in response to CEO directives to cut costs. The financial managers established new revenue and expense budgets within each criterion based on the revised sales goals.

Despite making these cost reductions, combined with reductions in sales goals and quotas, more than 67 percent of the companies reported that they'd failed to achieve their sales goals in 2010.

The participants reported their delivery against sales goals over the previous four years as follows:

- 2008   94 percent

- 2009   67 percent

- 2010   77 percent

- 2011   79 percent

From a low in 2009, there was significant improvement by 2011. The reports showed that sales leaders forecasted they would realize an average 84 percent delivery against sales goals/quotas in 2012. While these trends certainly point in the right direction for many companies, the results still fall 16 percent short of sales goals of what for many companies is an already reduced level. Some CEOs reported that their sales results were now only equal to where they had operated four years earlier, while others remained at lower levels.

In 2012, although companies in some industries experienced recoveries in the marketplace, others reported stagnation and decline. With the emphasis on cost control at an all-time high, boards and CEOs started to question the actions that sales leaders had taken in response to the experience of a downturn or changing markets and how they were planning to manage their sales organizations in the future.

Unfortunately, 84 percent of the CEO respondents in our study reported dissatisfaction with the actions taken by their sales leaders outside of directed cost reductions.

They felt that sales leaders viewed these changes to be sufficient and put little consideration into any other improvements that might be delivered. Within that 84 percent group, 92 percent reported having concerns not only about the time that was taken to make non-directed changes but also about the lag between the initial identification of a problem and the actual acceptance that the problem required action.

As a measure of those times between the identification and commencement of making the required changes, we reported the following according to quarterly action timelines:

- 19 percent started directed changes within the first three months.

- 27 percent started directed changes within a three- to six-month timeline.

- 38 percent started directed changes within a six- to twelve-month timeline.

- 16 percent started directed changes only after twelve months.

The CEOs in the 38 percent and 16 percent groups—six-plus months—felt that on reflection, their companies had lost considerable momentum through the slower response times or inaction, and this directly affected market share and/or profitability. This then required considerable change in their strategic planning. A further fallout from the slower response times was that some companies missed their sales goals; the CEOs believed that the delay in acting had taken a deeper-than-necessary toll on the morale of the business.

Many companies reported that, since late 2010 to early 2011, they had changed their focus from survival in the market back to growth. Company strategies now incorporated new products, the innovation of existing products, and the opening of new sales channels to take their products to market.

A further finding of the report was that 59 percent of the respondents reported changes in their product mix that was offered to the market. Within that group, 27 percent had begun taking new products to market that complemented their existing offerings, or they replaced redundant product offerings. The remaining companies had plans to release new products and offerings in the next one to two years.

Interestingly, for many companies, all of these actions were reported to be driven predominantly by business areas outside the sales organization. Any cost reductions emanated from the finance organizations, and product innovations came out of the marketing and research-and-development organizations.

Based on this research, it would appear that sales leaders benefited from the decisions that were made in other areas of the business—*changes that removed them from direct scrutiny as those changes were being implemented.* Many CEOs have experienced firsthand the difference between their own focus and priorities for the company and those of their sales leaders. That gap, no matter what the size, can have a direct impact on the company's financial performance, which is the ultimate measure of any CEO.

As part of the study, Sales Focus International canvassed the sales leaders' perspective in an attempt to provide CEOs with an understanding of the chasms that can develop within their companies in this respect. The sales leaders' actions and priorities will certainly provide foundations for a sales strategy and its execution.

The respondents reported that they believed their key pressures for 2012, 2013, and beyond included:

- Achievement of sustained or increased revenue

- Realignment of sales activities to match overall business objectives

- The existence of longer customer buying cycles

- Customers' increased scrutiny of offers

- Decreased customer loyalty

- Decreased sales talent loyalty

- Poor hiring talent pool

- Increased competitor activity within traditional markets

None of these key pressures were surprising, given the current market at the time. The next questions were: How were these pressures going to be addressed in the companies' sales strategies, and what disciplines and standards would the companies apply to strategy execution?

From a CEO's perspective, all of these pressures will have a significant impact on the overall profitability and sustainability of a company. They will have a considerable domino effect through operations and into the company's ability to plan and deliver its products and services in a timely and cost-effective manner.

The key pressures that the sales leaders identified demonstrate that the market may have fewer opportunities, and these will have longer lead times for those companies that focus on their existing customer bases. The diminishing loyalty of the customer base can indicate greater customer transience in the future.

For sales organizations that are correctly aligned to strategy, this will bring opportunities while transient customers seek alternative offers from the market. The sales organization's selling capability will be under pressure—but more with respect to its new business strategy and how it will be executed to support the sales personnel.

Sales Focus International advises that companies must review sales strategies and incorporate risk management strategies if they want to minimize the impact of these key pressures. A strategy to offset the challenges must be in place for each pressure point; if they are to have a positive impact on the business, those strategies must be deep enough to overcome these potential challenges. When this occurs, the role of the sales leaders within the company will be defined by the actions they take to address the key pressures, as well as the timing of those actions. The CEOs will direct that the sales leaders must deliver above-goal sales in the coming twelve months. For companies like yours, the time for error or slow implementation has passed.

Some sales leaders had already begun the development of three-year plans, with a focus on immediate sales performance improvement and results and having a well-planned and measured approach to the years that followed. These people represented just 12 percent of the respondents, however. A slightly higher number (34 percent) had developed sales strategies for the coming twelve months, but these strategies addressed the immediate concerns of the business and lacked foresight about the future.

A disturbing 54 percent had simply continued the sales strategies they had previously developed, even though these strategies were not delivering results—they contained minimal measurement and lacked the flexibility to adjust to market changes.

The sales leaders who did have strategies in place reported the following actions:

- Restart hiring   24 percent
- Change hiring criteria   6 percent
- Restart training and development   14 percent
- Revise metrics   5 percent
- Perform ongoing cost analyses   4 percent
- Realign sales structure   8 percent
- Revise compensation plans   26 percent
- Adjust sales goals/quotas   29 percent
- Install technology   8 percent
- Restore travel and expenses   27 percent

The study showed that the primary focus was still on sales goals, compensation plans, travel expenses, and hiring. The other strategies or actions had a much lower ranking in the sales leaders' priorities. SFI was surprised by the low ranking that was given to metrics and costs, since these are critical to strategy execution. The other stark finding was how little change had been made to both sales structures and hiring criteria. In other words, these sales leaders would be taking the same team to the field, with similar skills, to address the new economy; this approach was in contrast to the changes in the market and the change in customer loyalty they had experienced. Another notable finding was the low emphasis on training and development, even though the hiring pool had lower skills, and existing hires required education in the new markets.

The study concluded that the actions many sales leaders were taking would fall short of addressing the potential issues that lay ahead; many sales leaders would continue to rely on applying past practices to new and future markets. The degree of change that was to be brought about would be less than half of what companies were experiencing in the market at the time.

This situation is most concerning for CEOs, as their overall strategies and operations rely on sales goals being delivered. Given the cost cutting that has taken place in recent years, companies are thin on margin and require reliable delivery of sales goals to remain profitable. You as a CEO must consider intervening in sales strategies before your company loses further profits and market share through lack of competitiveness and timely action for strategy execution.

A critical function of the sales leaders' roles is their ability to identify not only the right changes to make but also the degree of change that is required to be effective. Any changes that are not correctly analyzed or identified (or that are not sufficiently deep to address the core problems) will put greater pressure on the business. With many companies experiencing pressure concerning cash flow and profitability, poor strategy and execution will be extremely costly to your business.

The skill that will be required above most others is the ability of the sales leader to identify and deliver those changes in the right sequence, and to do so in a timely and effective manner through the sales organization. Strategy execution has never been as heavily weighted in sales leaders' skill sets as it is in this era. Of the sales leader respondents in our report, just under 32 percent reported that they had experience in delivering change management projects through their sales organizations, and only 4 percent had experience in delivering complex change projects.

Each respondent was enthused by the opportunity to be involved in a change management project, and they all indicated that they would take the lead role. The lack of experience that is being applied to such a vital area of your business should be a further concern for you as the CEO.

In order to gain more understanding of the depth of the changes that they were involved in, the respondents were asked to describe their activities related to delivering changes over the previous twenty-four months, as well as the core changes they focused on. The 32 percent of respondents in this category reported the following activities as their experience in delivering change:

- Implemented customer relationship management (CRM)

- Increased the use of CRM

- Held more frequent sales meetings

- Revised sales call plans within territories

- Focused on top customers

- Implemented changes to territories

- Increased product segment focus

- Increased sales call numbers

These changes were delivered over a twelve-month period. With over two decades of experience in change management, SFI would rank these changes as "soft" changes, typical of normal sales function activity in the current market, and not as change projects. A degree of complexity would only be reached if all of these changes were implemented at the same time by a very entrenched sales force with a long-standing history in the business—especially considering the extended delivery timeline.

In reviewing the results of those change initiatives, the sales leaders reported the following outcomes in the eight change areas that had been identified:

- Number of changes planned: 4
- Number of changes commenced: 3
- Number of changes achieved: 2
- Number of changes measured: 1
- Number of changes delivered on time: 0

Clearly, these outcomes are insufficient for most companies if they expect to remain competitive in the market, and they highlight the need for CEOs like you to be diligent in how you identify, deliver, and measure change initiatives.

The question you then have to ask is: Do the sales leaders have the access to the knowledge and resources they need to fully understand sales force effectiveness and how to apply that to their sales organizations so that they will have a competitive advantage? SFI's research has provided CEOs with transparency on this much-needed knowledge and skill set. The proficiency of the sales organization will affect the company in terms of both profitability and revenue: how much sales leaders know about sales force effectiveness will be a key contributor to their proficiency.

The participating CEOs invited their sales leaders to participate in the sales force effectiveness segment of this study; of the 480 participating companies, 287 sales leaders responded to the sales force effectiveness analysis study. Of the remaining invitees, 129 company sales leaders reported that it was not relevant to their specific situation of sales force leadership, while 64 company sales leaders did not wish to participate.

The CEOs were certainly surprised by the lack of desire not only to participate, but also to gain further knowledge about their career skills. The sales leaders' responses were in line with studies conducted in 2009 by Dave Kurlan, a respected sales educator in the United States. His study found that:

- 18 percent of sales managers should not have been in sales management.

- 34 percent of sale managers were untrainable.

- 7 percent of sales managers were "elite."

In other words, Kurlan concluded that 52 percent of all sales managers—more than half—should consider doing something else…like selling. Sales leaders are closing the door on gaining knowledge. This lack of full understanding of sales force effectiveness for their organizations is creating an unnecessary chasm between their companies and their competitors.

For those participating sales leaders, respondents were tested on their knowledge about sales force effectiveness and the elements that contribute to it. The study looked closely at the relationship between sales force leadership practices, sales force effectiveness, and sales leaders' levels of knowledge and adoption. The measurement was applied using the sales force effectiveness model described in the book *Building the Most Effective Sales Force in the World: The Era Post the Global Financial Crisis*.

Respondents were asked to identify what they considered to be the number of categories that come into play in sales force effectiveness.

Among the 287 respondents, the results were as follows:

- 0 – 10 Categories   67 percent

- 10 – 20 Categories   22 percent

- 20 – 30 Categories   11 percent

Most of the 67 percent group could cite only seven categories, and those were related directly to the sales process (training) and CRM software. This reflects the overexposure most sales leaders have had to the term *sales force effectiveness* in marketing by training and CRM vendors. The sales leaders who cited ten to twenty categories included subject matter related to hiring, actions related to strategy execution, and sales tools and measurement. Those who cited twenty to thirty categories included all of the above and also had a strong focus on business, profit, and risk management. Their commercial skills were mature, and they held a broader skill set than their counterparts.

The respondents were then asked to identify the number of contribution points that supported all of their categories, which would be actionable points for change and sales improvement for contributing to overall sales force effectiveness. Again, the results were as follows:

- 0–30 points   24 percent

- 30–45 points   37 percent

- 45–70 points   18 percent

- 70–100 points   9 percent

- 100–150 points   7 percent

- 150–200 points   5 percent

These results were reflective of the categories. Sales leaders primarily said they relied on just forty-five action points to run their sales organizations and provide them with analyses for decision making. This is insufficient for running a highly competitive sales organization.

In fact, Sales Focus International's model of sales force effectiveness outlines 24 primary areas and at least 150 individual points as contributing to the effective conduct of a highly competitive sales force that delivers predictable performance and achieves sales goals. The number of points varies according to sales channels and industries, but a minimum of 150 are in place for most of the sales organizations in the study demographics.

There were clear differences in the ranking, and, as established in the book, many companies and their sales leaders at the time of the study used moderate interpretations of processes rather than full analyses of their correct application. We found that this was predominantly driven by sales leaders' limited access to knowledge and lack of education.

These results will have a serious impact on the performance of a sales organization, since they have a direct effect on:

- Identification of improvement areas

- Ranking of improvement areas

- Creation of change strategies

- Implementation of competitive capability

- Achievement of revenue

- Management of costs

- Execution of strategy

Some CEOs were contacted for their opinion of the overall results; their response was that they believed sales leaders would have gained this knowledge of their own volition and without a formal directive from the company. Clearly, this is not the case. CEOs like you must take action to ensure that sales leaders are suitably trained to deliver results in today's economies. Without correct analysis, you can expend considerable revenue in the wrong areas of your sales organization, which will have a direct impact on your company's top-line and bottom-line performance.

Having demonstrated their understanding of sales force effectiveness, the sales leaders were then asked to provide their perspective of their company's performance within the SFI model of sales force effectiveness. They were asked to rank themselves within three primary categories:

- 5 percent ranked themselves as "best" performers.

- 67 percent ranked themselves as "average" performers.

- 28 percent ranked themselves as "poor" performers.

All of the respondents were then required to rank their opinions of their sales organizations' effectiveness within twenty-four primary categories of best, average, and poor performers. Although some companies ranked in all three standards across the different primary areas, SFI applied a weighted average to arrive at each ranking. The participants were asked to validate why they had ranked themselves within each category.

Upon deeper analysis of their answers and validation, SFI applied our own rankings to the participants:

- 8 percent were ranked as "best" performers.

- 25 percent were ranked as "average" performers.

- 64 percent were ranked as "poor" performers.

This result demonstrates that few companies can be categorized as highly competitive sales organizations that employ sales leaders who have a full commercial understanding of sales force effectiveness and/or how to develop and execute sales strategy. This means that there is an enormous opportunity for sales leaders to take market leadership from their competitors by gaining the knowledge and application skills of sales force effectiveness and strategy execution when they are based on deep sales organization analysis and when a proper plan of improvements is established for them. Since CEOs are responsible for the strategic direction and profitability of their companies, this study supported the view that more scrutiny is required of this critical area of the business and how it is managed.

The results were consistent with SFI's previous findings that the overall level of talent in sales leaders was not increasing along with the demands of the market. We now believe that not addressing these issues could have a significant impact on the business in the form of lost profits, direct or indirect behaviors of the sales organization, and/or lost market share.

CEOs like you must minimize these risks and act to take maximum advantage of the new economy. You can accomplish this by taking the following steps:

1. As in other areas of the company, you as the CEO must implement more scrutiny and improved practices to increase profitability in the sales organization—through either lean manufacturing or other operational and financial best practices.

2. Now that the sales organization is under increased scrutiny, you as the CEO need to consider it alongside regular business practices, and remove your company from applying exceptions to this significant profit regulator of the company.

The sales organization's failed performance can have a catastrophic impact across the company.

3. Board members, directors, and CEOs like you need to minimize the risk in your companies by seeking third-party best-practice scrutiny of the sales organizations. You must seek hard evidence and facts rather than the traditional rhetoric that is applied to this critical area of the company. You as the CEO must not only have sales leaders who *embrace* change, but people who can *deliver* change and install best-practice standards across the sales organization.

4. CEOs like you must question the basis upon which sales leaders make their decisions about sales strategy and execution. You must review your company's strategy and execution practices to ensure their alignment with the company's overall objectives in both the immediate and distant future. You must review the execution plan for its application of business skills in establishment, milestones, and measurements. Because sales leaders can become the lynchpins to success for some companies, CEOs need to ask if their sales leaders are themselves willing to learn, change, and adopt new practices in order to minimize the risk for the company in unnecessary loss of profits and market share. CEOs must also examine whether there is hard evidence of them taking those steps.

5. Finally, as the CEO, you need to ask yourself if your sales leader is suitably qualified and experienced to identify and deliver the necessary improvements to the business. Does he or she require mentoring, skills education, or replacement?

This research report provided CEOs with some initial insights into their sales organizations and the potential risks, as well as an understanding of the quality of their sales leaders' availability in the market and those leaders' ability to deliver. It offered CEOs an understanding of the next steps they had to take to minimize risk and maximize profitability. CEOs like you who demand more will be best positioned to take market share and increase profitability and shareholder value. The table below provides a summary of the study demographics.

Table 1. Research demographics

Total participants	480 companies
Industries	Construction, importing, industrial, manufacturing, wholesalers
Sales channels	Wholesale, direct, distributor, other
Geographic area	Australia: 79 percent New Zealand: 12 percent Asia: 4 percent North America: 4 percent
Revenue	$10–$25 million: 12 percent $25–$45 million: 23 percent $45–$60 million: 43 percent $60–$100 million: 19 percent $100–$150 million: 3 percent
Sales employees	Fewer than 10: 2 percent 10–20: 17 percent 20–30: 29 percent 30–40: 26 percent 40–50: 22 percent 50-plus: 4 percent

Research Update

In 2015, the original review group of 480 companies were contacted and questioned for their sales revenue performance and their general views of their sales organizations. They reported the following rates of achievement of sales goals:

- 2012   84 percent

- 2013   81 percent

- 2014   79 percent

- 2015   81 percent

The CEOs said that the rapidly changing markets and the high level of competitiveness were taking a toll on their sales organizations and their ability to respond in a timely manner. Many of the initiatives had not gained sufficient traction to have had a meaningful impact on company performance. Many companies had returned to cutting costs in an attempt to retain profitability, but that was becoming increasingly challenging. Other companies' focuses had returned to operational efficiencies and effective fiscal management. Many CEOs mentioned their frustration with their sales leaders' performance.

The CEOs were convinced that they needed to take a new approach to their sales organizations.

04 The New CEO

The new CEO is looking at business through a new lens. He or she adds a focus on sales, but not in the traditional sense of sales.

Product-driven executives and accounting personnel often minimize sales, as they see it as no more than conversations and customer service. They view sales as the realm of big personalities and storytellers and high-cost individuals. They witness firsthand that the management of the sales division is often loose and somewhat unreliable with results, and that quite often it is managed more by customers' demands than by any purposeful management methodology or commercial practice. This has become the accepted norm in such companies, and the status quo of "That's just how sales is" transcends all decision-making activities to the point where companies manage risk into their strategy and forecasting endeavors to offset the known dilemma. Sales are unpredictable, unreliable, and fraught with escalating costs. In such companies, marketing is seen as the cousin of sales, with many similar traits.

Through the new lens, a CEO like you begins to see sales and marketing very differently. Sales becomes a manageable, predictable business unit that is commercialized to the point of being taken seriously through renewed reporting, measurement, transparency, and accountability.

Similar to the way in which manufacturing and logistics have undergone significant modernization and improvement to deliver efficiencies, reduce costs, and improve product quality, sales divisions are now front and center to that requirement, too. CEOs now see it as the *business* of sales rather than the *conversation* of sales. A CEO who is focused on the sales business will have greater control over the company's strategy being fully executed and in a timely manner. In such companies, the sales business delivers higher-than-industry growth rates and reduced costs that go directly to bottom-line improvement.

Quite often, the sales business is the last to receive the necessary attention so that it will be considered equal to operations, finance, and other commercially structured business units. The new sales focused CEO, in contrast, learns that the business of sales is not simply about customers and sales revenue; those are merely the outputs of many other activities and actions.

The new sales focused CEO peels back the layers and goes deeper into the drivers of the sales business, and he or she enables effective management of how the sales business operates. Such CEOs look at what causes or creates the two aforementioned outputs of customers and revenue; their expectations of sales leadership changes significantly, demanding a much higher level of accountability and commercial thinking. Rather than looking only at the two narrow channels of customers and revenue, CEOs like this have the ability to see the sales business from a 360-degree view. Looking only at customers and revenue can disguise issues, create alarmists, and corrupt the delivery of the strategy.

The new CEO gains an understanding of the intrinsic value that should be gained from the marketing business and how marketing is an extension of sales (or sales is an extension of marketing).

CEOs like this learn how sales and marketing are closely intertwined with (and are dependent upon) each other in today's world to deliver top-line revenue and increased profitability.

Some CEOs will say that they already focus on sales through constant reporting and conversations with sales leadership. I would question whether they go far enough, as my consulting experience and research supports the fact that most CEOs fail to have sufficient measures in place for identifying the early-stage alerts to looming problems in sales. They also fail to have sufficient measures in place to enable strategy execution to be planned, implemented, and delivered.

Seeing the business through a new lens does make a difference. I have seen this many times during the hundreds of business reviews I've completed across the globe. Unlocking the keys in each business enables CEOs like you to achieve far more than what others are delivering in their industries.

Why should CEOs like you focus on the business of sales and on changing the paradigms of how the sales and marketing business operates? Those CEOs who do so, deliver 50 to 80 percent more profit in their companies, according to McKinsey.

That is the reason and purpose for any CEO.

05 The Masking of Sales and Marketing Business Organizations

Traditional business thinking places CEOs like you in a position that hinders your ability to succeed in changing market conditions. We've all seen this over the past decade: CEOs became victims as market conditions became turbulent, new competitors arose, and the business environment became less predictable.

The problems and successes all start from the top. As a CEO, you have the mandate to set the strategy and vision, build the culture, lead the senior team, and allocate capital. You make decisions that affect the company as a whole, and you provide the leadership that keeps the company striding toward its strategy and vision. Senior leaders of business units report to you on managing finance, human resources (HR), operations, manufacturing, and logistics. (The exact mixture will depend on your individual business and the products/services you take to market.)

Each of those organization heads operates within agreed-upon functions and can be relied upon for his or her output. In finance, for example, there are "generally accepted accounting principles," or GAAP; such managers' functions are bound by software that supports those principles. In operations, there is "enterprise resource planning" (ERP) software, which binds how operations manages the back end of the business. Various governments have established ways in which human resources organizations are required to operate in terms of workplace regulations.

Then you look at the marketing and sales business units. Your marketing organization is renowned for its constant requests for funding, and often unmeasurable outcomes. Many companies are currently opting to cut marketing budgets when funds are limited, sometimes even closing down entire marketing organizations. Marketing is one of the first areas to be wiped off the list of fixed costs, since such a step can be done easily.

Sales, however—since it is accepted as volatile, often problematic, and the direct connection to the company's customers—will survive any downsizing. Poorly performing sales forces survive, while operations bear the brunt of lower-than-forecast revenue. Amid the general puzzlement that is sales, executives rely on the accounting organization to produce financial reports as the measurement of performance; measurements are often based on lagger reporting, with little to no data that would provide levers for successfully changing the direction of sales performance.

Some companies have advanced their sales business units to embrace customer relationship management (CRM) software as a method of forecasting, believing that this will remove the mystification of the future revenue that will come into the business. Many such companies are left disappointed, even if they can achieve adoption by users. Those companies that do achieve adoption quickly learn that the CRM probability factor associated with pipeline reporting is as reliable as gambling on a horse race.

Interestingly, CEOs often accept the forecast reports as problematic, and they look back to the reliability of the financial reports from accounting and forecasting based on customers' prior purchasing patterns. CEOs frequently find a sense of comfort in reporting that comes from an accounting source. The logic of this thinking is shoddy at best. No other business unit would be graced with this luxury of underperformance, poor reporting, limited to no transparency, and, most of all, a total lack of accountability.

It would be unheard of for your finance organization to fail to provide month-end or year-end reports that are accurate. It would be unheard of for operations to consistently deliver only 85 percent of planned output. Sales and marketing, in stark contrast, are cloaked with the idea that this is acceptable. They are high-cost business units with wavering accountability.

Yet the improbable has indeed occurred in the business world, and it is accepted to the point that board members, accounting, and even directors of companies focus the least (if at all) on sales. Some universities are now starting to resolve this problem, but most information that has been taught to date is two decades behind what today's market requires. Business schools still struggle to understand the business of sales.

The paradigm that must change is how companies view and manage sales and marketing, and how sales and marketing operate within the company. The responsibility of sales and marketing cannot be delegated as easily as that of other business units. Given the lack of commercially accepted structure, this responsibility becomes the greatest risk to the business. The delegation is often made to a person who has questionable commercial education and thinking—often someone who struggles to understand how to function in his or her role. Some 78 percent of such people should not even be in those roles, according to research by SFI conducted in 2009.

The masking of sales and marketing must be stopped, and CEOs like you need to be the catalysts for that change. We must see new thinking beyond the financial report.

06 Why Financial Reports Are Letting You Down

The most relied-upon tool for a CEO is finance reporting, created by both internal and external accountants: month-end, quarter-end, and year-end reports; cash-flow forecasts; and the list goes on. Managers and CEOs anxiously await such reports and then pore over them with the intent of making effective decisions for building the company's profitability. Recommendations for cost cutting fly around the room, and executives work vigorously not to have their costs reduced within their business units.

Those reports from accounting (and subsets thereof) are the core of conversations and, more important, how the company's performance is measured. The focus of such conversations is always improving profitability. CEOs meet with their senior executives to discuss business unit improvement and give these executives an understanding of their actions moving forward. Sales organizations gift-wrap their promises of improvement in stories about the market, the company's competitors, product issues, delivery issues, credit control issues and, of course, insufficient headcount.

The vulnerability to CEOs like you lies in relying too heavily on those reports to measure sales performance, since this financial information can be dangerously misleading. When your company is doing well, the conversations are polite and enjoyable; after all, what CEO doesn't love a day out with the sales leaders, since they are quite often great company?

When your company is seeing a decline—or worse yet, a significant drop—in sales, traditional financial statements can understate the seriousness of the situation because of the way in which unsold inventory is reported. Your company is not seeing or acting upon the early warning signs that are vital to driving growth. In such situations, conversations with sales become tedious and pressured, and you start looking to finance, not sales, for answers.

Herein lies the dilemma for you as a CEO: With standard cost accounting, you are initially rewarded by making more product and allocating it to inventory, regardless of whether or not you are actually selling it. Therefore, not only have you been lulled into creating more inventory to protect your income statements, but you are also lulled into thinking that when sales drop, you are not going to be affected as much as you really will be.

In many of my initial discussions with CEOs, a common point that we often make is the fact that they did not realize how deep the issues were within sales. The CEOs have typically waited longer than they should have to make decisions, since they were overly reliant on a combination of financial reports and sales leader representations. I have yet to hear a sales leader say to his or her boss, "We are going broke," as such a statement would be an indictment of that leader's performance. The worse the sales performance, the more likely sales leaders are to deflect the issues to other areas of the business.

This allocation of product to inventory is a blind spot that catches many good CEOs off guard. Those who wait too long and, due to lack of quality information, put too much trust in what they are told, can find themselves with a business that shifts into a kind of death role, with figures bouncing up and down month to month to the point of flatlining.

Another dangerous blind spot is that standard cost accounting obscures the line between fixed costs and variable costs, thus leading to poor decisions being made about discontinuing product lines and the cost of nonperformance in the sales business. Good product lines are often dropped from companies' offerings—not so much because the products do not have merit but because sales never bought in to selling them. Old lines are often continued well beyond when they should be because customers continue to order them, perhaps not realizing that the technology or offer is outdated. Finance reports do not give the true picture during such situations.

Most companies underestimate the impact of nonperformance in sales on company profitability. Profit is made in the last 20 to 30 percent of sales forecast revenue, not in the first 60 to 70 percent. Traditional accounting practices manage all costs as variable. Therefore, when a company loses $100,000 in revenue, the company accepts this as fine: "If the gross margin is 30 percent, then we've only lost $30,000." If the company is behind its sales goals by 15 percent, then it applies the same thinking.

This measure is incorrect. In reality, a lot of the costs in your business—your facilities, management, and staffing, as well as insurance and similar factors—are fixed, or they are fixed in the shorter term. You cannot change them in any reasonable timeline to match the changes in the top-line performance of the business.

A planned 30 percent gross margin contains your variable contribution to profitability based on a forecast level of sales revenue. When your company does not deliver that revenue, your variable margins might be more like 60 percent—so you lose $60,000 of profitability, but half of that loss is hidden.

All too often there is a disconnect between what accounting reports say and what is really happening.

The sales business affects profitability more than any other area of the organization, while operating with the highest risk factor. The problem for many CEOs is that they perceive that when they get their monthly reports, they have reliable information for knowing about the vital issues in the business and where increased profit can be achieved. Companies often make comparisons of past to current performance.

I would challenge that thinking. I can say from our experience that you cannot know the details of the sales business based on accounting reports alone. The levers for growth do not appear in either standard or nonstandard accounting: they function outside the common reporting disciplines that operate within a company. They are not a feature of any known accounting or CRM software reporting process.

When numbers are falling in the top line, companies often immediately focus on profitability. Production is scaled down, importing is slowed, and, depending on the degree of collapsing revenue, people will be terminated to address the shift in revenue-to-profit ratios. Such strategies will provide short-term solutions to the problem but will continue to conflict with the company's capability for delivering revenue. The levers of growth are not being measured or implemented.

The request for greater revenue is one that is futile; it explains why most companies default to cost-cutting measures. If the capability to win more business existed, it would be happening. I genuinely believe that most companies' sales forces are not responsible for many of the problems or issues that surround poor revenue performance. While they are an easy-to-blame group, in the end it is the managers who are responsible for revenue issues. Sales forces are a reflection of their management teams. No matter how much talent you have in your sales business, it will be for naught if that talent is mismanaged.

From a CEO's point of view, how you manage your sales leader will have a direct impact on the performance of the sales business; the same applies to the marketing business. In order to ultimately achieve what your company has planned in terms of strategy and profitability, you need to look at the business with a new lens to address these high-risk business units of sales and marketing, since they affect your company in every corner of its existence when they are not performing.

Only when there is a shift to a CEO who drives a very focused, energized effort and who relentlessly works with the right measurements, levers, and drivers can there be any kind of guarantee of the delivery of strategy and profitability. Such a shift is one of the most important things that can happen for any company.

When CEOs like you continually challenge and review these business units in a new commercial process, you will see a fundamental shift in the thinking, culture, and practices of your company. These business units will become more than revenue streams; they will be considered business units that experience consistent review for capacity, operational costs, and effectiveness of the business drivers that provide the outputs of customers and revenue. These business units will then make effective decisions based on business principles, and not just on customer demands.

High-performance companies are those where CEOs like you get involved.

07 CEOs Who Lead with a New Lens

The delivery of strategy is intrinsically linked to sales and marketing. Rarely does a strategy not rely on the performance of these two sectors in delivering revenue, profit, and the right customer mix in the right markets. If strategy is the function of the CEO, then strategy execution must be the priority of the CEO.

The strategy means achieving more than your competitors to gain more market share and placing the company in a winning position against some or all of your competitors. If you want your company to stand out from others, then like your competitors, you need to walk a different path. You need to think differently, see things differently, and—this is important—respond differently. You need to have the confidence and desire to excel beyond all others. Only then will you find a new lens through which to view your business: one that supports you in achieving what you plan; and supports you in making good, timely decisions.

Without those qualities of thinking, responding differently, and seeking new ways of viewing the business, you will deliver more of the same. You will remain connected to your competitors, duplicating them and responding in predictable ways. You will make minor changes, but most likely you will merely see distorted views of what could be and wrangle with elements of an ideal new world.

You will attempt to fit it into your old world, with the result that you will have a confused, unbalanced organization that is incapable of moving forward. I have reviewed many companies that have grasped onto ideas and concepts that have undermined the company's balance, which then causes different issues—often those that lead to sales downturns, since they have their eye off the real problems and are caught up in idealism.

For those who want to see the business through a new lens, the view must make sense and be grounded in business thinking; most of all, it must be based in common sense. The new lens brings new cultures, new leadership, new strategy, and new vision to a business. These are all the mandates of the CEO. The sales focused CEO is a more hands-on individual. This person is in marked contrast to the traditional CEO, who relies on financial information that flows up the management ranks and essentially flies blind. The sales focused CEO demands new reporting that has a deeper understanding of sales performance; he or she closely monitors the levers and drivers to ensure that the strategy is delivered and sales forecasts are achieved. Such CEOs make decisions on a more timely and insightful basis.

With the new lens, you will have greater insights into the sales business, thus providing you with a platform for improved decision making at all levels within the sales and marketing business. The alignment of the units creates a force in how the company goes to market and delivers strategy in a timely and cost-effective manner. The sales focused CEO works with new goals and targets, a new culture, and fresh thinking about ways to maximize the performance of this critical business unit. In order to enable the sales and marketing organization to prosper, he or she makes decisions that go beyond the scope of responsibility of individual sales leaders. Only a CEO has the mandate to make these decisions.

The change in how the sales and marketing business will operate is so fundamental that some things simply have to be decreed by the CEO. Consulting with management could take weeks or even months and could derail the intent and outcome that is necessary for the business to survive and thrive. Pressure to achieve sales often reduces the relevance of collaborative management, since the market demands decisions now.

The other challenge is that quite often the decisions related to new sales goals and targets; the metrics to be applied; and the structure, processes, and methodology, all require an understanding of the entire organization, not just the individual business units. Those decisions must come from the top down. If you attempt to engage in consultation, you will lose the fight, since they will give you a long list of reasons why you cannot do it. You first need to ensure that you have enough confidence in yourself as a CEO to take a stand and make the decisions that you need to make; then you need to focus your energies on ensuring that those decisions are carried through.

A sales focused CEO is one who has relentless follow-through on decisions, mandates, and actions and whose focus is transmitted through the senior managers who are on the front-line sales force. That is where the strategy is executed. Without that relentless focus, the sales leadership becomes a filter. Such managers will segment the requirements into one or more of the following: (a) requirements that are too hard to do; (b) requirements that they disagree with; (c) requirements that they will deal with when they have the time; and finally (d), requirements that they will actually act on. That filter is the most problematic in any business, and one that I see all too often.

When reviewing companies, the first item I consider is strategy. What does the CEO want to achieve, how many revisions have been made over the years to achieve it, and where is the company now on that journey?

In 95 percent of the cases, the strategy is sound; the issue is the lack of execution and the time it is taking. Upon review of whether or not the strategy can be delivered, the facts demonstrate that it can, but the human factor is simply not managed to do so.

Strategy and change go hand in hand. A good strategy requires changes in the business to achieve new customers, new markets, and new products. A strategy that is more of the same is not a strategy at all; it is simply the company's usual way of performing. A strategy is a set of initiatives that need to be delivered within a set time frame if they are to have the desired effect on the company and its market position. It is well known within lean initiatives that organizations where the CEO leads the lean "journey" (much like a strategy implementation) will realize far greater success than those that don't. Delegation of the responsibility has its consequences. Lean manufacturing guru Art Byrne states that only 7 percent of lean initiatives succeed, and those successes are directly due to CEO involvement.

The execution of strategy has many similarities to a lean initiative. Without CEO involvement, implementation will not be achieved. The required transparency, measurement, and accountability are invasive to this traditionally cloaked business unit, which all too often benefits from the murkiness that often masks sales leaders' lack of skills.

The sales focused CEO who looks at business through a new lens is the one who is best positioned to excel.

08 Your Personal Challenge

During your first two or three years as a hired CEO, you spent most of your time resolving problems that somebody else created. The first two years are when CEOs like you make the most sweeping changes, pulling the business around to the model and focus you need to execute your strategy. Five or six years down the road, however, there is not a problem in the company that is not your problem. If you run a privately owned company where the CEO is a director or managing director, you have a long history of management of the business. You have been through several metamorphoses to build the company to where it is today.

For all the things that are good or bad in any business, as CEO you created every one of them: some planned and maybe some unwittingly, but you have created them all. Some CEOs like to take a more backseat position when driving the company, while others like to lead from the front. Whichever style works for you is the one you should stay with, since that is the one you have honed your skills in, and the one that is going to support you the most in your decision-making abilities. Neither position precludes you from making great decisions promptly.

The challenge that you now face is in changing from a product-driven, focused, financial CEO to one who adopts new thinking and practices in an area that you are simply not as familiar with as you need to be.

That is where becoming a sales focused CEO can get a little tough, because you may have developed a methodology for doing business that has served you well, but now you need to extend that methodology further to deliver even greater results in the business—whether this means new markets, increased revenue, or (of course) increased profits.

Your company has certain ways of thinking, operating, and responding to situations; that is company's culture. There are the written guidelines, and then there are the unwritten expectations of how things should be done. You have created a culture in the senior executive team, and the conversations that everyone has support that culture.

Stepping into the role of a sales focused CEO requires you to change that culture and also change the language of the business along with the expectations of the senior executives. The sales leader is often seen as the one who will be most affected, but without a doubt, everyone feels the effects when the CEO changes direction or focus. Finance will produce different reports and will measure from a new lens, rather than the traditional, invoiced basis. Operations will provide different reporting back to sales, and the same is true for sales to operations. The sales leader will bear the brunt of most things, as that is where the greatest changes will occur. The marketing organization is a close second, as it will shift from branding and functionality to leading demand generation.

From a company point of view, your new focus on sales and marketing can raise levels of uncertainty and concern among your personnel. They will contemplate what the new focus will mean to them: Will this change be good for them personally? This concern can bring to the forefront many questions or issues you may not have been fully aware of. People's responses to crises will mean that employees will be pitted against their management, and they will exhibit poor morale and low productivity, even to the point of not trusting management.

For sales and marketing, the deflection of responsibility can escalate to near-unbearable levels. As a CEO, you will likely be met with threats of departure and lost customers, grandstanding by key personnel, and stories of doom as you indicate that changes are ahead.

Most people, by nature, treat all change as negative. A group of people can build on those negative thoughts if they're not managed correctly. I've seen many CEOs fail at implementing change because they made unrealistic, autocratic announcements about how the changes would assist the company and its staff. Such statements immediately propel people into adopting defensive positions.

As a CEO, you have to consider what this situation will mean to the business. How long have your workers been in the business? How good are they at coping with change? What is change to them? Do they see the need for change, or are they content with how things are currently going?

Underestimating the negative impact of change always has major consequences, and overestimation has very few. When all is said and done, the change you want is for your strategy to be delivered—and delivered completely—on time. And you want sales goals to be achieved so that the company will have the funding necessary to grow to the next level. That is a plausible and responsible reason for a change initiative.

The need to gauge how much change is required is a personal challenge in itself. Having the ability to objectively review the business and the people whom you have hired, managed, and worked with is a skill that is not taught in business schools, nor is it one that comes easily to anyone. Most people who lack this ability face the classic case of being too close to the forest to see the trees.

The other factors to consider are what the company should change to and what needs to be changed.

Too many companies make the wrong changes, thus further compounding issues in the business. Their view of the business is distorted, which leads to a lack of clarity that is so desperately needed before any CEO can embark on change.

In the final pages of this book, I present a case study that exemplifies the issues faced by a CEO when conducting an internal review of the requirements of his organization. The CEO's perception of where the business was traveling, and what issues it faced, were masked in the financial reports. During a growth capability review, I uncovered facts demonstrating that the business faced far greater problems than it had first considered, and that within a matter of months, for the first time in the company's forty-year history, it would be showing negative figures.

When conducting growth capability reviews, we can look to twenty-four contributing areas of the sales organization—and an equal number in marketing—that become catalysts to delivering strategy and profitability. They minimize the risks associated with this puzzling area of the company. Such a strategy involves knowing how to look at the business through a different lens, understanding the real behavioral traits of sales and marketing, and knowing what will be effective in changing its direction and capability.

Fundamentally, you will most likely need to take the following steps:

1. Change how the company completes sales strategy and implementation plans.

2. Install a management culture in which people are measured and rewarded for delivering all of their roles' requirements within a high level of transparency.

3. Restructure the sales organization so that it will be more aligned with the business requirements, and more balanced through the right behaviors and capability of the salespeople.

4. Increase the new business capability of the business in order to secure the right customers more frequently and in the right locations.

5. Improve analyses of accounts and business behaviors so that you can make more informed, timely decisions.

6. Install lead-generation marketing disciplines that are measurable and accountable and that will support buyers in today's market.

If these wholesale changes are not made, your business will face challenges in reaching its full capability. You need to break off the behaviors that are currently stopping the business from delivering strategy and exceeding forecast revenue. You cannot achieve change through casual meetings, with no structure or proper measurements. The strategy must be delivered through constant corrections of minor misbehaviors on a daily or weekly basis, rather than allowing bad habits to take hold. This means making smaller, more frequent decisions that will keep the business heading in the right direction. It also means understanding the broader impact of those decisions and keeping the view of the business and its operational requirements wider and deeper than what most sales leaders are comfortable with.

For example, imagine a sailboat crossing from one side of the Pacific Ocean to the other. You have a starting point and a landing point. Your best chance of taking a successful journey will come from making a series of minor corrections throughout the journey, rather than finding out that you are hundreds of miles off course and in need of major corrections to get back to where you need to be headed.

In my first book (published in the late 1990s), *Get Sales Focused: Rethinking and Revolutionizing Sales Forces and Sales Results*, I spoke about the need to have a moneymaking line. The moneymaking line is the carefully planned journey that your strategy takes before it is delivered. If you navigate along that line, you will succeed. The problem for most companies is that there is no line to manage or navigate along; they have a concept of where they want to end up, but they fail to map out the journey to get there.

As you can imagine, people must change with any initiatives and changes. As CEO, you must be comfortable with making other people uncomfortable if you hope to achieve results. You need to change the business philosophy to its core to achieve the change that will deliver the results you want. The entire business must be dedicated to change, and not just the sales organization. You need the business to adopt a new way of thinking, and the culture to be permanently embedded within it.

As a sales focused CEO, you need to have more involvement in sales and marketing. CEOs sometimes find it difficult to take a more hands-on function in sales, since they may fear that other areas of the business may suffer. The hands-on approach I'm referring to means having deeper reporting, having more informed conversations with sales leaders, and embedding accountability within your company. You need to lead people through the change, ideally through the management of the sales leader. If the sales leader decides that he or she is not up for the challenge, and you dive into the trenches and become hands-on early on, then you have to be able to pull yourself back out again in order for the company to move forward.

In order to deliver strategy and see the business through a new lens, we are ultimately talking about a sales and marketing transformation.

Organizations must go through a metamorphosis that occurs within a reasonable timeline and is commercially sustainable for the business. Typically, that timeline is less than twelve months; any time past that indicates that the company has either lost direction, or that leadership is not dedicated to the relentless requirements for change.

09 Mitigating an Elevated Level of Risk

Throughout this book, we have discussed the reasons that you need to look at business through a new lens. We've looked at the importance of your strategy being delivered, and the culture that supports that implementation. We have discussed the need for change and who is best positioned to lead that change. As CEO, your focus on change defines the company's success, just as it affects your choice of your improvement leader (2IC).

We now need to consider the elephant in the room: the sales leader.

Strategy, as far as this book is concerned, relates to revenue—specifically, the achievement of revenue targets, new customers, and new markets. These are the foundations for any growth. One of the greatest risks to any strategy is having insufficient revenue, commonly referred to as sales. Without due diligence being applied to ensure the delivery of consistent revenue and above-planned sales quotas, organizations will struggle to meet their demands each and every day.

For some companies, sales leaders are hired employees who are selected for their perceived knowledge and talent in leading sales organizations to deliver results. Such people are reviewed for their knowledge of sales, the industry, and the product, and emphasis is placed on their network of customers and associates.

Again, there is that sense of comfort that they will embrace values similar to that of your organization and thus deliver results.

Sales leaders are some of the most difficult hires to make. Why? Because most people have never experienced, met, or evaluated a top-performance sales leader. We have no real measure of what one is, and many HR departments fail to hire people who can deliver results. They seek a more focused and conservative profile that does not buy in to the usual rhetoric associated with sales leader interviews.

Many sales leaders are at best only capable of continuing the natural flow of the business, based on the momentum that is created through the product and brand. They deliver very few initiatives that will have a lasting and positive effect on a business. When the brand/product begins to exhaust itself, they quickly become the custodians of a failing sales organization. They will make traditional, low-impact attempts to improve results through sales training, territory realignment, or customer reallocation, but they will not make sufficient changes to the trajectory that the business is now on.

Failing sales leaders cause much pain to a company; interestingly, such leaders will focus their attention on job retention more than growth strategies. This means that their personal interests outweigh those of the company. CEOs often misunderstand the conduct of sales leaders during this phase: the sales leaders work vigorously to build personal relationships with key people in the business in order to build safety nets around them. As discussed in an earlier chapter, "The Masking of Sales and Marketing Business Units," CEOs can find that a lack of commercial thinking and business practices is being applied in their organizations.

Failing sales leaders can have several far-reaching effects on the organization:

1. Financial:

Financial expectations are missed when the sales leader fails. This can result in the loss of bonuses for the executive team and budget cuts across all organizations. For listed companies, this can also result in the loss of shareholder value in some cases. This underperformance places you as CEO in the spotlight, as it is the first reported problem to be closely aligned to falling profits. Whether you are a CEO of a publicly listed or private company, this is the most exposed area of the business, and the ramifications reach far down the line.

2. Costs:

The lack of external process to the market is reflected directly in the internal processes that are applied to the sales organization. This results in a high cost of sales and many indirect losses through inefficiencies, similar to those experienced in production areas. Companies carry excessively high costs, as referenced in the chapter "Why Financial Reports Are Letting You Down." As the sales revenue collapses, the direct and indirect costs will escalate rapidly. When this process goes unmanaged, it can quickly become a zero-profit year in a company's profit-and-loss statement. CEOs do not want failing or collapsed profit reports on their résumés, since this will immediately devalue these individuals in the market.

3. Customers:

Customers are poorly served when the sales leader fails. Salespeople are left to develop their own way of operating in the field, and often resort to serving low-hanging-fruit customers or those with the least resistance to access. An enormous number of opportunities are left unexplored when sales leaders are "hands off," which is often masked by statements such as "Focus on the top ten, twenty, or thirty customers." These are your company's most loyal and easily accessible customers.

They contribute a large proportion of the operating revenue, and accounting divisions see them as the only customers of value. They require the least skill and effort to retain. In many cases, they demonstrate that a company is inwardly thinking and not outwardly growing.

4. Competitors:

Competitors benefit from a failing sales leader, since many accounts are not suitably protected, and the sales team is often disconnected from other offerings in the market. Companies often suffer from an overreliance on a few top performers to deliver results, which leads to escalating wages to retain top producers, and cutting prices to keep top customers. Competitors respond quickly to company failures, since they provide them with great stories, and also instill fear in customers who don't wish to risk dealing with your company. Once that knowledge leaks into the market, it will gain its own momentum, thus increasing the trajectory the sales leader has put your company on.

5. The Field:

The level of talent of field personnel diminishes quickly when sales leaders have failed, as they now have no mentors and little training or personal development. Companies often pride themselves on the duration of the field personnel's employment, rather than on the talent of the individuals. The team has vastly fluctuating skill sets; this situation is more reflective of what they brought to the role than what they gained through their employment with the company. Although stability in personnel is often deemed to be a good thing, in sales it's the opposite. The enemy of any sales organization is complacency, and salespeople become complacent quickly when their sales roles shift from selling to nurturing customers.

Most CEOs' immediate reactions are to attempt to stimulate the sales team through training and motivational offers. The sales team represents the effect of the problem, however, and not the cause. Focusing on the field team does not resolve the problem, which is coming from the top sales leader down.

Each and every one of these five impact points of the business goes to the core of a CEO's responsibilities—including shareholder value, costs, profitability, market share, and customer value. CEOs are at high risk when their sales leaders fail. Identifying the early stages of failure can reduce the risk, but only in cases where the CEO gets involved. This is where you come in. Some of the warning signs may include your sales leader demonstrating one or all of these traits:

- Dealing with the issues as they arise in the business, rather than dealing with them in a systematic manner

- Objecting to external reviews or opinions

- Rejecting training, believing little value can be added from it

- Not measuring the strategy or the strategy-execution plan

- Not improving the performance of the sales organization

- Becoming reliant on the company's legacies and on "hero" salespeople

- Not delivering change; the business model is somewhat stagnant, even though all markets and competitors are shifting rapidly

The average tenure of a sales leader in today's market is ten years; many of those people are actually failing at their jobs. The other side of the coin has to do with high turnover rates (less than eighteen months), as companies struggle to break through the legacies of longer-term incumbents.

SFI conducted research in 2009 in which we identified that 78 percent of sales leaders lacked the capability required to deliver growth during changing markets and economic conditions. This situation places any business with such sales leaders in a high-risk situation. A sales focused CEO (like you) is the person who can change the trajectory of the company in the short, medium, and longer terms. A hands-on CEO who works closely with the sales leaders, and within a structured and disciplined culture, will mitigate this high level of risk.

When a CEO takes the lead, on the other hand, the outcomes can be significantly different from situations where sales leaders are left to operate with minimal reporting and structure. When this happens, sales leaders respond to business demands and do not operate in the typical autonomous environment they may be used to. They are accountable, and are required to advise the CEO as to why they make specific decisions, the foundation of the facts they rely on, and what effects this will have—both within and outside of the sales or marketing business. There is a level of transparency in such situations that underperformers will not enjoy, since sales focused CEOs like you do not enjoy underperformance.

For you, as a sales focused CEO, the change in these core points will be significant. Let's look at those same five factors again, this time when a sales focused CEO is in charge.

1. **Financial:** CEOs who drive sales improvement and growth through the transparency of the sales leader's performance will create financial prosperity; this will mean that new projects will become funded by surplus profits. Sales focused CEOs understand that it is crucial to drive the sales leader to perform to a plan finding a replacement or accepting status quo. It sends a strong message of accountability throughout the organization.

2. **Costs:** The organization will improve its internal efficiencies in cases where the sales organization has an impact on the company's broader audience. This situation will have a direct benefit on EBITDA (earnings before interest, taxes, depreciation, and amortization).

3. **Customers:** Customers will be better served, and more customers will be added to the company through focused efforts. The growth of the company does not rely on organic growth, but rather on a balance of both existing business and new business. Key accounts in such a situation will be well protected through sound management practices.

4. **Competitors:** Sales focused CEOs will improve the performance of the entire industry. They will bring forth new standards, innovations, and opportunities, thus establishing the company as a market leader.

5. **The Field:** The talent in the field will be more productive and effective through focused management and ongoing development programs. This situation will reduce the internal cost of sales. These employees' skill levels will be reflected in customers' accounts and will be demonstrated through their ability to grow the business and increase the value they deliver.

Making sales leaders accountable, and implementing new measures for improved decision making, are integral to the delivery of your strategy. The pool of sales leaders who could potentially deliver and accept the new culture will be smaller, but those who do, make noteworthy contributions to the business. Those who are looking to rise in their careers will be drawn to CEOs like you—that is, those who prioritize sales along with the associated discipline that goes along with that strategy—since they will personally derive immense benefit from such discipline.

Those who are not capable (or desirous) of participating should be let loose early so that no time will be wasted. People will make their own decisions regarding engagement, and the role of the CEO is never to talk them into doing so. At the senior executive level, you require voluntary engagement at all times.

10 Selecting the Right Improvement Leader

As a sales focused CEO, you have a few considerations to make about how you're going to make the transition, both personally and in the business. As discussed, shifting to successful strategy execution means change—change that requires you as the CEO to lead the initiative—but you will require a strong leader on the front line to make that happen, day in and day out. As CEO, you must avoid getting dragged into the trenches by having the right improvement leader (2IC), to deliver.

When you assess a potential 2IC, you need to look at the requirements for the role. The 2IC will have a major impact on the business, and the last thing you want is to have to carry someone or to have a conflict with that person. This person is pivotal in your quest to become a sales focused CEO. When you announce any change initiatives in a business, you will be flooded with suggestions of who can accomplish this, and people will put their hands up from both within and outside sales and marketing. Often, the sales leader or a marketing leader has attempted to address certain issues or implement initiatives with little to no success; in some instances, these people may be the problem, not the solution.

Some people view new projects as exciting opportunities—especially change initiatives. They often see change as an opportunity to do things differently, gain higher positions, make their marks, and potentially earn pay raises.

Naively, many CEOs expect that all that is required of them is to "manage the people" and "have them focus on the tasks." Right?

Unfortunately, this simple approach demonstrates why more than 70 percent of change projects fail. They take too long to deliver, thus making them irrelevant, or businesses tire of the change processes and overthrow them. CEOs get pulled in different directions, and other priorities take precedence over their initial intentions.

Change leaders are unique individuals who operate outside of the team, meaning that they have few relationships with existing team members. They are objective and possess the skills that allow them to transcend the issues and deliver success. They have specialized skill sets that enable them to manage people successfully and lead them through complicated processes. They do not become battle weary, and focus relentlessly on the front line to make change happen. Successful change agents have honed and perfected their skills over many years by implementing change projects. The more rigorous the change for your company, the more important this functionality becomes. Implementing new measurements and levels of accountability is all about people, not process.

To assist you in understanding the best person to be your 2IC, let's consider the following as a functional test. As you read through these criteria, make mental notes about whether you have someone in mind who possesses the described skills and attributes.

1. Profile of the change leader:
If change leaders want people to follow them during changes, they must have the respect of those they manage. These types of leaders must set perfect examples of the way things are going to be, and they must not be seen as people who only give lip service or teach from a book. Change leaders are action-oriented people, not teachers.

2. Trust:

Trust is a critical factor for success. If the team does not possess trust, the people on the team will lack commitment, both to the 2IC and to your objectives. Further, you need to ask if any of the potential 2ICs' past actions raise any suspicions related to your intentions. That is, have any of your current or previous actions or functions placed him or her in a negative light in the view of the employees?

3. Role clarity:

The potential leaders have a thorough understanding of the subject matter and have previously demonstrated that they have paid their dues. Such people have experience with changing roles and can show empathy for, and an understanding of, different issues. The advice they offer will seek to solve issues while maintaining a commitment to planned outcomes. Ultimately, you may ask: Does their involvement add value, or will they be seen by the team as only managing a process?

4. Excellence:

Implementing a transformation requires that a potential 2IC show commitment to sales and marketing excellence. This is an area of study that, when applied, serves to establish a competitive advantage. This person's understanding and commitment to this methodology will have a critical impact on the successful outcome of the change.

5. Problem or solution?

Preconceived opinions of others can limit potential 2ICs' abilities to drive change. Do the people involved see them as successful advocates, or as part of the problem? This situation is further pronounced when sales leaders lead the change, since their previous involvements may have tarnished their credibility.

6. Can the 2IC stick to the plan when the going gets rough?

The change process is always tumultuous and will prove more difficult as the project progresses; ingrained cultures will exacerbate this problem. The team will likely not be receptive to the change process, and its members may reject it altogether. Quite often, the skill gap between what the company requires and its current level of attainment will demonstrate the degree of change that is needed to meet the company's objectives. Does your potential 2IC have the resilience to keep going during the change process—no matter how difficult, painful, and frustrating this might become?

7. Does the potential 2IC know the rules?

Quite often, a set of rules has evolved over long periods of time that are unique to the team. If potential 2ICs have come from different areas of the organization, they may be completely oblivious to the existence of these rules, or may lack insights into the ways to negotiate through them. These types of rules have evolved culturally, and the potential 2IC may find that the rules have not been documented. These unwritten rules will either support or hinder the change you are implementing.

8. Get ready to move quickly:

Rapid change is more likely to deliver results than slow change; the change leader's experience and the executive's dedication will determine the velocity of such change. Change in a sales environment can prove to be explosive, since personalities often clash. Because change is not a voluntary, "nice to have" experience, your potential 2IC should expect to encounter resistance at all stages of the process.

9. People before process:

The bottom line is that companies do not implement change projects because of new systems, processes, territories, or structures; they implement these projects because of people's inability to adapt to using those systems or processes.

Change projects are about people, and people are complex. Change will only occur when people are committed throughout the different stages of the change; only then can a company realize the results of revenue improvement and mark these results as a successful change or transformation.

Leading change is not a matter of being liked or popular; in fact, it is a matter of being able to manage people even when the leader is unpopular and disliked. Has your potential 2IC successfully led people to change over a sustained period of time? And has this experience included intensely traumatic times that involved loss of power and prestige—or even employment? Has this person made tough calls as far as terminating people, and has he or she been the person to deliver the bad news?

10. Systems:
The challenge for change leaders is to get the systems, processes, and structures right. Does your potential 2IC understand the complexity of what is required of him or her? Does this person understand the levers that are required to drive results, and the systems that are required to support the change? Systems go well beyond just a CRM; they involve the tools that the company requires for planning, managing, measuring, and making decisions that occur outside the CRM. These systems form the fundamental basis of a successful sales transformation leader. Does this person have those tools, and are the tools custom-made for your company?

Choosing a 2IC is an important decision that requires considerable thought before making any engagements. You may have identified someone in the business who will be your ideal 2IC, or perhaps you can see the benefit in having someone from outside come in to assist with the change process. When the company is settled into the new processes, this new person will make these new processes the new culture of the business. Because each business is unique, each case requires a deep understanding of what to change and who will be the 2IC of that change.

11 Getting the Management Methodology Right

With the careful selection of your 2IC, you must consider the managers on the front line who are leading your sales force. They can be state- or region-based people—some with solely sales responsibilities, and others with state office responsibilities, including sales. Whichever they are, they will have a great impact on the success of your business. They are the people who have the day-to-day communications with the team.

We have spent some time in previous chapters looking at the traits of sales managers or sales leaders, as well as their shortcomings and strengths. We have looked at how those on the front line respond to issues and challenges, and how they cope with change. The research I discussed earlier has provided several excellent insights into the trends and behaviors involved, and has highlighted a few areas of concern: specifically, sales leaders' slowness to act on change, and the fact that they make minor changes that will have little to no impact on the business. Their propensity for autonomous management means that they will undergo substantial personnel changes while attempting to manage the team in a more structured environment.

If you are hiring for this front-line role, a natural reaction is to contact the people you know from your network; there can be a certain sense of safety in sticking with the known when you need to make changes.

This could be the most destructive method you can apply, however, since it means that you're trying to fit the past into a new world. The people you actually need are completely different from the people you have experienced in the past; they must have new skills, capabilities, and focus.

The hiring process often goes like this when you're embarking on a change or improvement: The first person you approach or consider is often a collaborative manager. You see this person as someone who has the tactics and style necessary for easing your company in the right direction. Your team will respond to this more gentle approach, and this will encourage their engagement. Rarely have I seen this approach work in sales organizations, however, since you as the CEO have a finite timeline for getting things done. This management style does have its place in companies that have natural momentum in the market, and in cases where the salespeople are more customer service related. The hiring of such people is an expensive learning curve for CEOs of most organizations, though, since these people often rank well with HR management.

The next approach I often witness is where a CEO hires a veteran manager who was very good at the sort of accountability culture that is often thought to be the main requirement for sales improvement. This type of stronger management style is less forgiving and more focused than the collaborative manager type discussed above. This kind of manager is a bit of a dinosaur in today's market; such people often use the approach of setting numbers for the month and then demanding answers when the team fails to attain those numbers. This type of person is an authoritarian from the old days of commission-only selling environments. This sort of approach disengages the team further and creates a deeper culture of "us versus them." As the CEO, you can feel confident that this kind of manager is focused on team performance, but this is simply not the right type of focus the team needs.

The challenge that you face as CEO is that in both situations, the business is most likely getting worse by losing traction, and that is the one thing you need to get moving. I've seen companies operate for months (even years), flicking back and forth between these different management styles; companies sometimes even bring past managers back in order to achieve some comfort and relief. The past is the past, however, and you must not go back there. The sales focused CEO requires a new, contemporary, fresh-thinking person who will embrace new practices in sales management.

The management methodology is pivotal to your success in growing the business and delivering strategy, and that is where I focus my efforts. There needs to be a very careful balance of:

- Respect for the employees, since you need them to be engaged in order to deliver results

- Structure without stifling creativity

- Processes that get salespeople thinking

- Tools that assist them in controlling their destiny and outputs

- Accountability for the delivery of the outcomes

- Coaching to assist those who need improvement

- Clarity with respect to performance requirements

- Management of the culture of the business at the team level

- Management of the individuals and their contributions to the culture

- Acknowledgment that difficult decisions will need to be made, if required

- Rewards for those who do achieve

- Encouragement for those who need it

This communication style requires a mature-minded professional who has commercial thinking and patience. This person knows where he or she needs to go and engages everyone on the journey, thus gaining high-quality contributions from each and every person. This management style does not occur by chance, however, and will certainly not happen without the right tools, systems, and processes being in place. I can also tell you that this style will not occur without a sales focus from the CEO.

Given the importance of the 2IC and the front-line sales leaders, I have a very standardized, specific way in which we at Sales Focus International manage sales teams. We have tested, improved, and used this method widely over twenty-five years of turnaround consultancy; and it delivers revenue improvement in three to four months. It includes all of the tools, systems, and processes that CEOs like you need for the right management style to prosper. When this system is in place, it is incredibly powerful.

We developed the methodology to this point only after we'd learned the power of getting managers to understand these principles, and then allowing them to work through the various processes before asking their teams to do the same; this approach is so powerful that the teams are then heavily invested in the methodology. This is a methodology that you will not attain by sending managers to a course. I've trained thousands of sales managers across the globe (young and old), both in classrooms and through online training; their training is never to a level that matches what they get from being part of a business and being guided through its processes. In the classroom environment, managers typically pick the "nice to have" points and leave many of the "need to have" points on the table. The problem is that people will not engage at the level of detail that is necessary to make it work. When they're working with the methodology in the business, the detail becomes part of the process, and then they have to use it.

The glue that holds all of this together is the management methodology itself. While the methodology itself is not particularly complex, the consistent application of it is what takes time. It is those first few days invested that can be the "make or break" of how easily a company will adapt to the new environment.

Learning how to drive the management methodology and how to support it can be difficult. Companies want to change things, but they often lack an understanding of what they're really changing or what the longer-term effects of the change will be. Once the initial indoctrination is complete, the change must be mandated by the CEO if it is to gain traction.

The methodology has to do with performance, and the output that individuals achieve. Some will excel, while others will underperform. Rarely does a sales team excel every day; it will always have ups and downs, according to its pipeline velocity. This can mean that red and green will appear all over the reporting, which is a simple yet effective measurement process.

For management, the question becomes how to manage those days of red and turn them back to green. This is a matter of accountability, but it's not about shaming the people involved. They can feel the shame themselves just by the reporting format; you do not need to drive it home. While accountability is very important, it is not what most people think it is. It does not mean setting goals and then shaming those who don't hit their numbers. Accountability means making sure that everyone understands where they're trying to go and knows how to get there; it means asking them about the levers they can pull to change their outputs and then staying close enough to them so that they'll do the things they need to do to get you there. This can change from week to week or from month to month, which means that you need to stay close enough to them to coach them through the process.

Leaving a person to sink or swim, as is often the case in autonomous management regimes, contravenes the intent of the management methodology. Much like in a mature, lean organization, it is a given that managers and team members need the right tools and clear guidelines for their activities if processes are to be successful. Furthermore, managers in lean organizations count on their superiors to assist them in removing any barriers that stand in their way.

The sales focused CEO must ensure that the culture of his or her company supports these same principles and methodologies throughout sales and marketing. The systemic removal of any barriers that prevent sales teams at all levels from succeeding is also necessary. Firefighting duties, nonrelated projects, and wasteful activities (such as unnecessary paperwork) can prevent managers from spending time supporting and coaching their people. Lack of knowledge can be the biggest barrier of all when managing people. These deficiencies are far less obvious than, for instance, the lack of a sales kit for a product, yet they are equally as debilitating. As a result, creating an environment where managers can succeed in a predictable way is one of the most challenging tasks for a sales focused CEO like you. These challenges often persist, even in companies that have had considerable success in improving their operations.

12 You Simply Don't Have the Time

Two types of CEOs have been combined into one for the purposes of this book. The first type is the owner-operator CEO, or managing director. This person is the classic business hero who, on any given day, may be found solving production problems, negotiating with suppliers, dealing with regulatory bodies, sorting out personal issues, hiring new personnel, making sales calls to customers and, of course, personally handling customer complaints. In companies where the CEO wears multiple hats, the management system is conversational in nature and relies on a high level of interaction with the CEO. The dilemma here is that much of the company's success may depend on the leader's unique knowledge, talents, and relationships. When the job gets too big even for the larger-than-life CEO, then the danger—to cite a phrase popularized in Michael Gerber's *The E-Myth Revisited*—is that management by delegation can become management by abdication. Sales forces often enjoy this style of business unit, and many people know little else than abdication and autonomy.

The other type of CEO is the hired person who leads a company, often reporting to a board of directors or several directors of the company. Such people are required to report in a more formal fashion, and, as discussed earlier in the book, they tend to rely on financial reports.

No matter which type of CEO is considered, the size of the company will dictate how hands-on the CEO is in the company.

Some CEOs will stay a little longer than necessary, since they enjoy the interaction "down in the trenches" and feel that they add value. Both CEO types are reactionary to any activity within the business and to its customers.

The sales focused CEO methodology is designed to remove the CEO from the day-to-day, reactionary decisions and to get him or her out of the trenches. The goal of this methodology is to become a strategist who monitors the delivery of the strategy from a high level—someone who has the ability to drill down quickly and easily to the on-the-ground action of any individual, and to do so at any given time if it seems necessary to do so.

In both profiles, the CEO is starved for time, and we all know that new methodologies and systems are renowned for taking up more time. If you find yourself feeling overwhelmed, at some point you might ask, "When am I going to have the time for all this?" This is a little like opening Pandora's box and learning about all the evils of the sales business that have been hidden from you for many years. Some CEOs simply close the box and forget that they ever saw it. Others know that the time has come to address it, but where do they find the time? Their calendars are already full, and the thought of even more being added can be overwhelming.

We could simply say, "Since it is such an important part of the company's success, you just have to make the time," but that will not solve the problem; it simply tells you why you need to do it, rather than telling you how to find the *time* to do it. The key is not to add to your time; it is to use your time more wisely. Becoming a sales focused CEO does not involve becoming more hands-on or doing jobs that others should be doing; it means managing sales and marketing more closely, knowing what to expect, and having the right information at your fingertips so that you can make good decisions consistently and in a timely manner.

Your time involvement in sales may decrease for any of the following reasons:

- **The sales focused CEO has shorter meetings:** CEOs who are not focused on sales often sit and talk with sales leaders at random times. The sales leaders are engaging, and often great conversationalists, and you gain direct feedback on the market and competitors when speaking with them. As a CEO, you will have more organized meetings that take less time.

- **The sales focused CEO uses improved reporting:** Once you're focused on sales, you will have reports at hand that will give you transparency and reporting on the things you need to know. You will deal with exception-related issues, not generalizations. You will have the ability to drill down deeper on any specific point you need to know.

- **The sales focused CEO has a strategy execution plan:** You will have a plan in place that demonstrates at any given time if you are on or off track for delivering what you have planned.

- **The sales focused CEO makes more decisive decisions:** You will save time by not having to dig for answers. The company's newfound transparency will provide insights into various trends, and you will be able to see the direction in which all the levers of growth are heading. This will allow you to make sound, timely decisions for problems.

- **The sales focused CEO deals with smaller issues:** Issues that are typical to sales will not escalate, since you will have more transparency, and timely and consistent information. These factors will ensure that the sales leaders are focused and proactively managing their business units.

- **The sales focused CEO deals with marketing that clearly demonstrates ROI:** No longer will you be blinded by obscure, meaningless reporting of Google Analytics, clicks, and other function-based reporting. You will have reporting that clearly demonstrates the quality of leads that are generated to support the strategy, the value of any business gained, and the quality of the decision makers who are engaged.

The intent of all of these factors is to reduce your time and increase your access to meaningful measurement, reporting, and information that will allow you to make decisive decisions in a timely manner.

13 The People Make the Difference

When shifting to becoming a sales focused CEO, if the entire focus is on tools and hitting the numbers, the shift will not sustain itself. Many companies have proved this by making short-term wins, only to then struggle to keep their people engaged. Being a sales focused CEO is not just about numbers—it is about people, too. When things are done correctly, a sustainable model will emerge that will become a cornerstone of how the company operates, which will shape the culture within the company.

In the highly competitive market in which we now trade, it is impossible for any one person to have all the answers. Sales focused CEOs are those who install frameworks that allow the collective thinking and contributions of people within their organizations to be channelled in the right directions so that everyone will benefit. The goal of such frameworks is to have the people within the sales and marketing organization become smarter when going about their roles. This will create an environment in which contemporary practices are embraced, which will then lead to the building of an invincible force to take to market. The old model of people operating independently and acting in response to their local markets is a thing of the past. In the new model, people understand the strategy and their individual contributions to it, and the collective experience of everyone creates an energetic approach to execution.

Large corporations have certain boundaries that define how people operate, since having boundaries is the only sure method for ensuring that large numbers of people will be productive and task oriented. Each area contributes to the overall motion of the business on a day-to-day basis, and each cog fits neatly into the next as the motion goes around. The challenge for this kind of culture is that people are not asked to think about what they're doing. This system is a dumbing down of the people; although they may be easier to manage, such a system fails to utilize the talent within the corporation. This represents an enormous waste of talent.

A sales focused CEO like you still needs to put some boundaries in place and provide clarity with respect to functional role requirements, but you set those boundaries with the intent of enabling creative thinking that will contribute to making a smarter company each and every day. You will use the collective energy of everyone, and will then channel that energy to where it will best contribute to the desired goals of the strategy. In these circumstances, all employees understand their contributions and where they can add more value to the process.

As a sales focused CEO, you create a culture where employees identify a problem and its root cause and then ask themselves what the options might be. This is an approach similar to lean thinking.

Sales and marketing managers usually find it difficult to give up their traditional, reactive roles and to shift their focus to coaching and supporting their people. Such managers often give lip service to the idea that they're coaching sales organizations, but rarely have I seen such coaching actually taking place in a proactive manner. Instead, any coaching that does take place is ad hoc, unfocused, and typically unresponsive to problems. Such activities are not a part of the culture of the business, nor are they preferred functions of such managers' management styles.

This situation becomes obvious when managers assert the desire for salespeople to be autonomous, which is the direct opposite of a coaching environment. Salespeople who act autonomously are not those who will adapt to coaching, whether for short courses or on an ongoing basis.

Strategy execution requires people to be on the same team: working and learning together, and being smarter about how they perform their roles. Only when that teamwork occurs will your strategy be executed. That culture comes from the top down. Your sales 2IC is going to play a major role in making this happen and becoming absorbed into the fabric of the sales business; the same will apply to the marketing business.

Many leaders require a new set of skills to manage such a changed culture. The act of leading people to find their own solutions involves striking a delicate balance. You need to be assertive and empowering at the same time, you need to have absolute clarity about what the final goal is, and you need to allow the people in your company to find the best and most direct course of action to achieve that goal.

A strategy does not need to be complex; it does not have to consist of pages and pages of information and explanations. For sales businesses, you just need to keep it simple. For example, you could aim for:

1. Sales revenue of $100 million in year 1, $125 million in year 2, and $150 million in year 3

2. Customers in x, y, and z markets, with a mix of 40, 30, and 30 percent, respectively, in those markets

3. A product mix defined with each stage of the life cycle

From this point on, the people in your company will have the structure, tools, and conversion that brings about the "how" they need to achieve the company's goals.

They will complete the process in a detailed and documented manner that will demonstrate that the final result is achievable.

Confident leaders will engage the people in their company and will investigate problems with them. They will inspire the people to find solutions and not simply dwell on negativity. Those who wish to engage in the latter or fail to engage with others need to be sidelined quickly. Jim Collins, the author of *Good to Great*, talks about getting the wrong people off the bus as quickly as possible. Lean management, with its similarities to business improvement, has also seen a rise in this thinking.

The business cannot pause and wait for people to adopt the right attitudes. *Skills* are not important—*attitude* is important. People can learn skills, and the processes assist them on their journeys. Companies often fail to deliver strategy and sales goals; they become overly focused on fostering environments where nonperformance and lack of engagement are managed through nurturing, believing that the company is obligated to assist such people.

This is a highly debatable point, but within sales organizations, each day that a person fails to deliver will affect the broader company, since that person is not bringing in revenue. If such people have no desire to improve within a commercially realistic timeline, then they have determined their futures through their own actions. It's time for them to step off the bus. Getting them off the bus contributes to the culture of the business and allows those who *will* contribute to engage with like-minded people; working together, they will build even greater momentum and energy in the business.

The people make the difference, and you want like-minded people working in your company.

Companies that are led by a sales focused CEO will have the capability and thinking that will deliver growth. This does not mean improving by just 10 or 15 percent; it means improving this year by 30-plus percent and the next year by 30-plus percent. This means challenging the company to be smarter, bringing new products to the market, and maximizing sales revenue. As a sales focused CEO, you will achieve the best return on your people resources through efficiency, and in being smart about how you go to market. This approach will compel your team to take a highly disciplined approach to understanding the strategy, utilizing its assets, and planning out its delivery process.

14 Why Strategy Execution Fails

Many of the strategic plans I review are sound and make good commercial sense. What I also see is that companies often attempt to deliver these plans several years in a row but simply cannot seem to get them off the ground.

One company I reviewed had a mantra of "30/30/30," which was an internal reference to achieving certain items within certain timelines. This plan had failed to the point that it had become a cultural joke, and no one believed that it was required, necessary, or achievable. No one had the necessary skills for delivering the strategy: not the people on the front line, the management, or the leadership. They had gone down unexplored paths, burning through huge sums of time and revenue in the process. People were involved in tasks that they should not have been involved in, to the point where one sales leader actually wrote an internal CRM system rather than using an off-the-shelf system. His time would have been better spent in defining ways to execute the strategy.

The bottom line is that many companies simply don't know how to implement the strategy, whether it is within sales, marketing, or other areas of the business.

This leads us to wonder where does strategy start and where does it fail.

As a CEO, you've thought hard about the business direction for the years ahead; you've done your research and have made the necessary inquiries. That information is then sent to the executive for his or her input, improvement, and innovation. Your company now has an agreed-upon strategic plan that is well researched and innovative and that identifies core actions for the coming years.

The next step is to take that strategic plan from concept to reality. In order for your plan to succeed, however, you rely on marketing to build the brand and open the doors. The sales force must then deliver the top-line revenues, margins, customers, and product mix you have planned. Unfortunately, you may have found that they have failed to do so; if this is the case, you are not alone in finding your strategy execution challenged.

In fact, according to a 2013 *Economist* Intelligence Unit report, in a survey of 587 companies across the globe, 61 percent of respondents admitted that their companies often struggled to bridge the gap between strategy formulation and day-to-day strategy implementation.

So why does strategy go wrong? Strategy execution requires two contributors: marketing and sales. These two business units are renowned for being out of alignment with each other. They are frequently rivals who compete over which group is more important and which one leads the way in influencing the revenue for the company. These points can be debated endlessly, since each company is different; it depends on the maturity of the business, the goals in the strategy, and the buyer process that engages with the company.

Marketing and sales do have two distinctive functions, however. Marketing sets out the company's brand, products, and services, and the sales team communicates the competitive advantage.

That positioning sets the direction for the sales team and provides them with the understanding they need so that they can communicate with customers in a meaningful way that will generate business. The marketing function will extend to contacting prospective new customers and generating leads for the sales organization to pursue.

The communication of the strategy to the sales force is typically done through a presentation to the team, the provision of some new materials to support the team, and the assumption that there will be the same level of buy-in that the authors of the plan currently hold. This information is merely the tip of the iceberg; the salespeople need more than that if they are to succeed. The traditional, conceptual approach to strategic execution is its first and major failing.

The sales organization certainly needs leadership to deliver, because when left to their own devices, salespeople will tend to wander aimlessly through the market, visiting their best (or most approachable) customers and selling the products that they're most comfortable with. They will be busy, and they will make plenty of "noise" as they go about their days. What they sell, however, may not be what the company had planned.

As the salespeople head down their own path—a different path from the one that was set out in the strategy—their defense is often that they are bringing in revenue (or at least close to the planned amount). What they fail to understand is that the mix of customers can be problematic, since they will not serve the company in the future; worse still, the salespeople may be signing little to no new business.

The conflict of sales and marketing then escalates, since marketing struggles to understand what has happened and what the team is doing. They do not see evidence that the strategy is working. The salespeople struggle to find their way back to where they need to be, and most often remain at large until the end of the financial year.

Poor leadership will affect the sales team, since poor leaders will lack the levels of communication and measurement that are required to bring the sales team back on track. This brings to mind the expression "herding cats." The team wanders aimlessly wherever its members want to go, much like a bunch of cats who have wandered off; if you've ever tried to lure home a stubborn cat, you will get the message in this story.

Poor leadership and poor communication of the strategy are not the stand-alone causes that will corrode strategy execution. Other contributors may include some or all of the following points:

- **Lack of buy-in:** When strategy means change, it's important to get people on board and assist them in seeing how the strategy will increase their job security and the likelihood that they will get promoted and see pay increases in the future. Companies often overlook this factor, which then becomes a greater problem when people do not understand the larger picture of what the company has planned and what their individual contributions will be.

- **Hidden agendas:** This is a particularly difficult problem to identify and overcome. Everyone has unexpressed thoughts and concerns; we all have egos to protect (some greater than others). Companies often fail to identify any unsaid needs or draw out any hidden agendas, since people are often concerned about alienating or threatening others.

- **Lack of momentum:** The company has failed to identify the real momentum in the business, and the company's strategy is a much greater stretch than was originally anticipated. That stretch is one that is too great for the team, as the members lack the skills to deliver the planned outcomes.

- **Passive management:** This type of management is characterized by the assumption that things will run themselves after they've been started. This is about as likely as winning the lottery three weeks in a row. When the implementation phase begins, if there is not enough follow-up from the CEO and 2IC, poor and inexperienced management will be left to execute the plan. Passive management occurs when senior executives fail to assign and hold individuals accountable for delivering on project points. No one takes complete charge of the process and relentlessly follows through on the details throughout the year. This requires a competent person to define the strategies, plot out the course of action, and manage others so that they will deliver.

- **Poor or incorrect motivation:** The question that all salespeople ask is, "What's in it for me?" This is not to imply that they're all a bunch of selfish, greedy, self-serving individuals (although others in the organization might certainly have those beliefs about them). People's motivations are complex, and a poorly written compensation plan can certainly undermine any good strategy. The sales team needs to not only buy in on the strategy, but also understand how the salespeople will benefit by delivering it. The more behavioral change that is required of individuals to achieve the strategy's goals, the more they will look for rewards. Without those rewards, they will continue to do more of the same from previous years. You are creating customer-service personnel, not sellers.

People overlook the value of incentives for salespeople, many of whom are expected to work for fixed-salary packages, just like any other employees. Such a situation is at best an idealistic dream for sales forces that work in opposition to growth and achievement; it can be the cause of dissent among other employees.

Executives often believe that salespeople are overpaid, and yes, some are indeed! If the top-line revenue does not come in, however, then you may need to open your mind to some of the contributing factors for that; lack of compensation or incentives may well be one of them.

Compensation defines the sales team's behavior and the members' hunger for new business. Even if the culture in the business has been one of loyalty and team spirit where everyone contributes, that will carry your company only so far. There will come a time when that loyal and positive culture will shift to one of "How much more are we expected to do for the same money?" If your competitors offer rewards and you do not, then you may be unwittingly leaving the door open for departures.

When you offer incentives to salespeople, these incentives have to be real, achievable, and timely payments that are easy to calculate and manage. Salespeople need to answer three important questions:

1. Are the rewards worth the effort?

2. Will better performance lead to greater rewards?

3. Will more effort lead to better performance?

If they answer yes to those questions, then they will put in more effort, which means that you are increasing the likelihood that your strategy will be delivered. A well-designed incentive plan that is carefully aligned to the strategic plan is a valuable tool that will contribute to strategy execution.

- **Lack of an operating plan:** This is seemingly obvious, but is one of the biggest failings of many companies. A sales strategy is the operating plan for the sales forces. Such a strategy allocates resources effectively and efficiently and serves to increase revenue and reduce selling costs; it focuses salespeople on the right targets, with the right degree of effort, thus enabling the team to deliver the desired outcomes.

The salespeople must have confidence that the plan will work; this is accomplished through coaching them in how to implement the plan in their territory, or customer profiles. CEOs who wish to minimize the risk of a failed implementation need to have the right components of the sales strategy measured and reported. This is not simply a matter of numbers; it is a matter of where the numbers came from and how they were achieved.

- **Lack of individual sales plans:** The process of planning does not come naturally to many salespeople. Many of them operate mainly within autonomous environments, where they make decisions on the fly and trust their gut instincts. These behaviors foster knee-jerk reactions to customer demands and requests; most notably, salespeople tend to sell on the path of the least resistance if they are left at arm's length by their management. If the sales leader does not manage their performance according to plan, each and every week, then the likelihood that the salespeople will head in the wrong direction will be high. Given all the battles in today's marketplace, a good leader is necessary for keeping the sales force headed in the right direction and for assisting them through the many challenges of selling in today's competitive market. In order for the results to come in, the salespeople must have the right conversations with the right customers and at the right frequency.

Strategy execution is like a project plan. The purpose of any project plan is to define the parameters and purpose of individual business units. For marketing and sales, such a project plan is vital: it clarifies why the plan is being implemented and the ultimate purpose the plan will serve. The plan serves as a central point for keeping everyone associated with the project on track and focused on the same details and information, and it provides a clear basis for measurement.

Sales and marketing leaders must present their CEO with a well-articulated and cogent strategy that demonstrates alignment between both business units. The plans should demonstrate, in concrete terms, the origin and method of revenue; the behavioral requirements; any resource requirements; and the risk management, implementation, and measurement plans.

15 Writing Sales Strategy

Benjamin Franklin once said, "If you fail to plan, you plan to fail."

How many times have you seen this sentiment written or referred to? More important, how many times have you seen a sales business unit fail to plan…and then fail as a result? Is your sales leader the type of person who jumps in a car and heads in the general direction of where you want to arrive, and then, when he feels that he's close enough, looks on the map to see where he should be? Or is your sales leader the type who sits down and plans the shortest, most effective route that will avoid traffic delays?

My personal observation is that most sales leaders jump in the car and rely on gut instinct to arrive at the destination, and they only check their progress during the last few miles, once things have already gone wrong. That is also a direct reflection of how they manage their team and the strategy. They have a general idea of what is required, and they just start off into the year, essentially continuing from where they were last year. In the second quarter, they tell stories when they're questioned; in the third quarter, they tell even better stories. In the fourth quarter, they make statements and abundant excuses.

The defining question then becomes: Which CEO bought in to the excuses, and which CEO refused to accept them? If the sales leader had the chance to live another year in your company, then you bought in.

Writing sales strategy is a fundamental requirement for proving to not only the CEO but also to the sales leader that the sales strategy can be accomplished. It is an indictment of the management of any company, and the board of directors, not to demand a clear document that demonstrates how the revenue will be achieved. As discussed in earlier chapters, a failing sales leader will have a far-reaching impact on the company and is a high-risk individual. Although the primary function of any CEO and board is risk management, this risk is often one of the most poorly managed risks in any business. Managing risk is a vital piece of planning that, if done correctly, can reduce costs and ensure that your strategy is delivered.

Quite often, this type of planning has never been presented to the CEO, since there is an unwritten sense that the plan is idealistic; very few people can say, "I have a documented sales strategy from my sales leader." In fact, in twenty-six years of consulting, I have yet to see a quality risk management plan (although that may be due to the nature of the consulting I do). What I do know is that sales leaders are experts at "selling" themselves out of doing such undertakings as planning and completing certain tasks. If the CEO has forced their hand and they have made an attempt, it is all too often lightweight, lacking in substance, and in a PowerPoint presentation format. The contents of these substandard versions may have touched on predicted account spending or some form of product analysis, a few selling statements on how good things will be, and a few points on the things that are potentially blocking the plan from being delivered. All of these points seem to tell you as CEO that the company is the best in the market at what you do. These plans—or more like sketching on a slide—do not provide any real benefit to the company in terms of strategy execution. They merely document the natural momentum that occurs in the business and demonstrate to you as CEO that this year will be more of the same as last year.

The challenge for you is that you have probably never seen a real sales strategy; therefore, it's hard to judge what one should look like. There are many common misconceptions out there about what constitutes a sales strategy, and Internet search queries will only produce hours of reading and cloud the subject further. My company defines sales strategy in this way:

> *A sales strategy is the operating plan for the sales force. It allocates resources effectively and efficiently so that they will serve to increase revenue and reduce selling costs. It leverages your sales personnel, thus fostering high-performance behavior and a world-class selling organization.*

As discussed, sales strategy is first and foremost linked to the overall company plan and the marketing plan. The sales plan defines which products and services are required to be sold, which markets penetrated, and the channels to be utilized. It also articulates the practical application and overall objectives of providing a road map that will guide the team in the best way to achieve their targets.

The sales plan must be the test of whether or not the strategy can be delivered within the nominated period (typically, one year ahead). Does the business have sufficient velocity, and does it have the capability required to deliver what is on the agenda of the strategy? Both of these areas undermine even the best sales strategies. I have often seen very ambitious and logical strategies that would have required entirely new sales organizations to deliver them. To that end, you must consider the degree of change that will be required.

Writing sales strategy is a matter of business excellence, which is commonly described as "a framework that is an integrated leadership and management system…[it] describes the elements essential to organizations' sustaining of high levels of performance."

High-performance sales organizations do not just happen by chance. They are the result of careful planning, as well as hiring the right people who will align strategy and the marketplace to deliver the required results.

There are five components to sales strategy excellence. Applying each of these components sequentially will underpin the plan and ensure your organization's success.

Step 1: Customer Segmentation
This means understanding the market, accounts, and buyers, including both new and existing buyers. This is not just "gut feeling" or judgment-based decision making. People often believe that they know the answers to this step based on their industry experience or longevity in the business. Their view may not be right, and often I find that they look to old models that are now dated, and at products that are reaching their maturity.

The selection of market and buyers must be based on objective and factual information that is not clouded by internal views. This is best conducted by the marketing organization through external providers in order to gain the right information. They will then be in a good position to write profiles for use in the sales strategy, develop the subsets of customer profiles, and identify the mix of business that will be required for protection and acquisition.

This step also ensures that the sales strategy is differentiated from the competition while being aligned with buyer needs, the corporate strategy, and the product strategy. This step is a precursor to effective planning.

Step 2: Planning
Using the segmentation findings from Step 1, your company should now develop revenue quotas/goals, customer plans, and new customer acquisition plans; once these are executed, they will allow the company to meet its financial objectives.

Your company needs to define the products that will contribute to each of those customer segments and maximize the sales of a product based on its maturity in the life cycle. This establishes the company for longevity while also meeting its short-term goals. As part of the planning process, these definitions assist in establishing the metrics of what is to be measured, as well as the frequency of the measurement. Measurement should focus on methodology and behaviors, not just on financial outcomes.

Step 3: Engagement

Next, define how the sales team is going to behave while interacting with prospects and customers, while also identifying the frequency levels and decision-maker levels to target. A clear understanding of these factors will define the requirements of the sales organization.

Step 4: Sales Organizational Chart
An effective strategy will require a change in the sales organizational chart. Unless you plan to repeat the prior year and achieve growth only through customers who are increasing their purchasing, then you will need to make changes to the organizational chart. Strategies that are competitive and that take market share require change; you need to make sure that the sales force structure is correctly aligned so that the right people are in the right roles to execute the various processes.

Step 5: Execution
Finally, communicate the strategy to individuals. and have them demonstrate how they will perform their roles. Execute the strategy by focusing on areas such as sales enablement and adoption, pipeline/forecast management, reporting, and so on. The sales leader must assist the salespeople by supporting them, coaching them, and creating fluidity between the marketing and sales business.

The devil is in the details. Even the grandest project depends on the success of the smallest components. Each of the above components requires thoughtful consideration; you must pay attention to the complexities within each. A plan that is well written and then filed on the server, buried deep amid other planning files, is not going to be delivered; instead, it is an exercise in the process and a starting point for business excellence. That excellence, however, is only achieved upon delivery. The detail of how each of those steps is completed is paramount, and the measurement of all the performance drivers is essential.

16 Early Warning Signs of Derailment

Because many CEOs miss the early warning signs of looming problems, they often deal with issues that have gained traction and need more time and effort to remedy. Those early warning signs go unnoticed for those CEOs who keep themselves at arm's length from the issues. How many times have you had a problem arrive on your desk, only to find out that the problem has been festering for six to twelve months? The unit manager has attempted to resolve the problem unsuccessfully, and now you have a major crisis on your hands. It will cost your business a lot of time and money to resolve a problem that may have only required minor adjustments if it had been handled correctly earlier on.

Sales and marketing are filled with early warning signs to which you need to respond. These two organizations are the first line of defense to the market, the first line of attack to competitors, and the first place where many companies feel the change in the wind.

Relying on the sales leader or marketing leader to actively monitor those changes is fraught with risk, because their accountability and obligation are often not equal to that of a CEO. Therefore, as CEO, you must continually monitor what is happening in your company and pay close attention to indicators that go beyond sales goals alone.

Early warning signs can be identified through:

- Lower responses to marketing campaigns

- Changing decision-maker profiles responding to marketing

- Marketing reports focused on branding, not lead generation

- Fluctuating, often low, deal sizes

- Diminishing margins

- Fluctuating sales results from the team

- Lack of standard operating processes
  (salespeople all go their own way)

- Sales results that rely on a few individuals rather than the team

- Inaccurate sales reporting

If one or more of these indicators is occurring, then you need to start asking questions and obtaining hard data to find out what is happening. What these indicators mean is that a strategy has gone off track and that the market is pulling the business, rather than the business driving into the market. The business has lost its rudder and is being pulled in different directions—and not in the direction of your strategy.

I have always had a rule of thumb with business that has assisted many companies in understanding the degree of the issues they face and the time it will take to resolve them. The rule is, "If your business goes off track for one month, it will take two to bring it back in line. If the business is off track for a quarter, it can take two quarters to pull it back in line." The sequence of the timing stays the same; the only way to shorten the remedy time is through a major intervention.

As a sales focused CEO, you need to constantly monitor for those early indicators and identify them in the first month. You then must ensure that they're resolved within the following two months. As discussed throughout this book, the marketing organization is charged with customer segmentation and ensuring that the company's products and services are aligned to the right buyers and markets; they set the scene for sales to be productive in talking with the right people and the right products. Marketing is charged with the responsibility of generating leads.

A marketing organization that has derailed takes the company down a very rocky and expensive road. Disconnection with the right customers and the market can have devastating effects on the company in both the short and long term. Monitoring marketing closely is an important function of the CEO.

Sales leadership is charged with the responsibility of making sure that the salespeople target the right customers, introduce the right mix of products, and achieve the right sales prices. This is where the plan implementation process becomes critical. If the implementation is not measured by the sales plan, then you can quickly find yourself with an entire sales force that is headed in the wrong direction. For many companies, the lack of auditing of marketing and sales means that salespeople will sell too much of the wrong product, at the wrong price, and to the wrong customers; not surprisingly, the strategy will fail. Revenue may be coming in the door, but the company is shifting further and further away from its planned goals. That shift may see the company lose market share or fail to grasp opportunities that it could leverage in the future.

The proper reporting can place a CEO like you in the position of monitoring the right indicators and, therefore, being able to make inquiries and establish causes before minor issues have a chance to balloon into full-blown crises.

17 Reducing Costs from Sales and Marketing

Reducing costs is often associated with a poorly operating company in need of finding profits—quickly. Successful companies know that cost reduction is an ongoing process and one that requires vigilance at all times. Such companies consider cost reduction to be more like waste reduction, which is a common misunderstanding with lean principles.

When people were first exposed to lean principles, most executives heard "cost cutting" when they saw the term "waste elimination." When the executive looks only for cost-cutting measures, she or he overlooks the other substantial benefits and gains from the implementation of lean and similar disciplines. While cost cutting is done on profit-and-loss reports, waste reduction is achieved through review and analysis of where improvements in processes and capacities can be achieved. Waste elimination does not always mean cutting costs; some costs can increase, but the output increases tenfold in comparison.

If you ask most sales and marketing leaders what the costs are for their business units, they will tell you about travel expenditures, training, hiring fees, and headcount. Marketing will bear a large proportion of the cutbacks, losing budget allocation and often headcount. Few sales leaders have been trained or exposed to efficiencies in sales forces that have sustainable and meaningful methods of operational cost control.

Marketing personnel are similar; their advertising budgets typically get slashed, particularly given the new emphasis on digital marketing.

In the research cited earlier in this book, CEOs reported that they had given directives to sales leaders to reduce costs in the following areas:

1. Compensation plans   64 percent
2. Hiring   76 percent
3. Travel/entertainment   54 percent
4. Headcount   41 percent
5. Goals and quotas   26 percent
6. Sales operating expenses   37 percent
7. Sales cost   29 percent
8. Training and development   12 percent

These are all obvious and easily accounted for through profit-and-loss statements. The reductions are focused on fixed costs and a few variables. What they do not focus on is the endless waste that occurs during the normal day-to-day trading of the business and the maximization of the salespeople's efficiency. Efficiencies are often related to the number of sales calls they make or to their closing ratios. These factors may account for part of the efficiencies, but it does not stop there. Countless attempts have been made to apply lean thinking to the sales process, and in my opinion, they have failed miserably. I have yet to see a version that has made a significant difference to a business. Being lean is a process of thinking about the business, the customer, the product, and the service. It is business thinking and not just a singular process within a business, as is the case with sales processes.

I focus my attention on the business and on waste elimination: eliminating unnecessary tasks (especially unnecessary repeated tasks), unnecessary errors, and of course, capacity planning.

The best way to explain this is through an example of an Australian company I worked with several years ago. The company was expanding rapidly across Australia through acquisition, government funding for manufacturers, and sales force activities. The business was on a roller coaster of growth and seemed unstoppable. It had created its own energy in the market, to the point that its salespeople were adding no value outside of being customer-service personnel.

Profitability was an issue, even with all the funding the company received, and it was necessary to look deep into the business and see where profits could be extracted. The company had made the necessary cuts through the finance organization's recommendations, but more still had to be done. Upon review of the sales force from a waste perspective, it became apparent that there was massive leakage in how it operated. All that passion they had for the product was coming at a price: that price was losing an additional $4.6 million out of $50 million annual revenue, and unnecessarily. The company processes were dismantled and rebuilt to contain the leakage and to put the additional profits directly toward the bottom line.

Where was the leakage coming from? We found several sources:

- **Unnecessary tasks:**
  Salespeople were involved in numerous tasks that they should not have been involved in, including the obvious ones such as doing deliveries, picking up payments, swapping trial equipment, and merchandising shelves. They also performed tasks related to the operational side of the business at the factory level, where they were called in to assist in stocking tasks, preparation of deliveries, outbound customer calls about deliveries, and supplier pickups. The business had a frenzied urgency to it—similar to what you see in many small businesses—where everyone was assisting everyone else.

Although this camaraderie might be considered a good thing, it keeps the business focused on the bottom 50 percent of tasks and not on the top 50 percent—where the money and profits are made.

- **Unnecessary repeated tasks:**
  Product and application knowledge were requirements for the salespeople, and one central person held the knowledge. The level of telephone calls to this one person was extraordinary; different people asked the same questions many times over. The lack of a centralized knowledge base or product information created bottlenecks while waiting for answers. The salespeople became so addicted to the calls that they would make them to ask minor questions instead of figuring them out for themselves. It became the culture in the business to telephone this one person for information.

- **Unnecessary errors:**
  The frenzied culture of the business and the constant telephone calls created excessively high errors in customer order documentation, internally processed orders, and factory orders, such that finance had to generate a high level of credit notes. The errors were further compounded by the fact that some sales personnel still used legacy product codes.

- **Capacity planning:**
  The field sales force was overstaffed, while the internal sales area was understaffed. This was relatively easy to identify based on the waste that occurred in the business; the capacity-planning analysis quickly ratified the observation.

This is an example of waste that derives from the old belief that salespeople manage the customers to the point that they become customer-service representatives on wheels. The lack of systems, discipline, and expectation of performance in the company had people taking on tasks that they preferred to do rather than the ones that needed to be done. People were unnecessarily handling things many times over, which caused some things to be handled two, three, or even four times more than they should have been.

Sorting out these points then allowed for deeper analysis of other areas of waste related to direct and indirect costs within the company's operational areas. This was as simple as providing reports to salespeople proactively as an information source, rather than their spending inordinate amounts of time calling the factory with questions about the location of their customers' orders. The analysis then considered the use of marketing tools, time spent on report generation, and the value of those reports.

At the end of the day, salespeople are hired and paid to speak with customers in a meaningful way that will move the business forward. Any tasks or barriers that reduce the time for having meaningful conversations are a cost to the business. These costs do not appear on profit-and-loss statements and will only be identified through process analysis.

One of the most interesting phenomena of the reviews that I carry out for companies is that most carry excess field sales force numbers, even though they always state that they are understaffed. Through a process of capacity planning, it is possible to apply math to the sales force and thus establish the real headcount number that is required. If you consider the repercussions of the excess headcount, your company is carrying unnecessary salary costs, insurance, tools such as electronic equipment, and a car for each person. This can vary according to the role, function, and level of seniority, but they all have a cost to the business.

Capacity planning can also align your resources correctly with your customer base, which can bring about an improved cost of sales. Your company can make the right changes that will ensure that the customers remain well serviced, if not better serviced, and that their accounts will grow. As part of capacity planning, you need to consider several questions:

- How much effort really goes into each customer and transaction?

- Which services do each of them need?

- What are the real profit margins on individual customers?

- Which customers and markets are growing, and which are shrinking?

The sales force can actually become better and less expensive if organizations reject certain traditional practices, such as assuming that larger customers need or want extensive sales coverage, and that the more calls you make, the more revenue you produce. Neither of these are true in today's new business world.

Capacity planning has another interesting offshoot that most companies initially struggle to reconcile. When I have applied this approach to sales forces and have made cuts, the opposite of what is expected occurs when the other right conditions are applied. As an example, I recently cut $1.6 million from a declining business in sales-related salary costs, and the company immediately saw an upturn in sales revenue. This was equivalent to a 2 percent cost cut that went straight to the bottom line; this improved cash flow and was critical to getting this business out of its problems.

The other side to this is that capacity planning means paying attention to opportunity—identifying the resources you already have in place that can assist in lifting top-line revenue. In these scenarios, I have delivered increases in revenue of 30 to 50 percent in short time frames by using the excess capacity correctly.

Depending on your business situation, both are good outcomes. In some areas, good savings can be made, depending on the go-to-market strategy of your company.

For many years, marketing and sales have been at odds with each other, both operating with high costs, and both passionate about their respective contributions. This disconnect between them leaves a chasm of cost escalation that must be removed. For instance, marketing will generate as many leads as it possibly can, as that is part of its mandate in the business. Marketing's view of leads differs from that of the sales organization. Marketing might nominate a lead such as the name of a person who showed interest in something by signing up for a blog, downloading a white paper, attending a free seminar, or writing a comment on a blog or social-media piece. These are all signs of people knowing that your company exists, but they are not leads. Marketing can spend an extraordinary amount of money, both directly and indirectly, creating "noise," which means that people are aware of your company's existence, but they are not actually engaging with it in any meaningful way.

A quick Google search will yield a plethora of information to satisfy the most information-hungry person. You may be seeking answers to your questions, or you may be generally interested in a subject. You may not be purchasing, or you may have a sufficiently annoying problem that needs to be resolved. You are just looking. Today's world is full of people who are just looking, and it is easy to attract noise. A great example is Facebook. Many times you will see a page go up on a topic that people are passionate about. You will see a high level of interaction and comments and "likes," and it may appear to be the most important subject on the planet. Ask the people who physically attend rallies about the many they've attended in the past where two or three people stood by themselves on a street corner waiting for their Facebook clickers to arrive. This is noise.

The Internet is the new face of retail. Many people are looking around, and if questioned about their interest, they respond with "Just looking," just as they do in retail stores when they're browsing. Salespeople who call those names that are given to them by marketing often receive the same response of "Just looking," and the people have a polite conversation before scuttling away. You can try a few fast sales tactics on them in the conversation, but often that only leads to a quicker exit.

A company can invest enormous resources in creating noise within marketing, but it is not going to support sales in a meaningful way. You, as the sales focused CEO, must focus on what the marketing organization is going to achieve.

The sales organization's view of a lead is a person who has contacted them and has demonstrated an interest in communicating with them about their company's product or service. If marketing and sales are focused clearly on that goal and fit any of the criteria below, then you have some cost reductions to make.

- The marketing organization's efforts are not attuned to attracting, engaging, and inciting people to make contact.

- Marketing is generating noise that potentially has a high cost, for a small offering of leads.

- Salespeople's leads have a very high closing ratio, thus lowering the overall cost of sales.

Marketing has become an integral part of the sales process today, penetrating further into the sales process than ever before. The department is no longer there for creating awareness; any marketing person who is focused on that is problematic. With the rise of content marketing enthusiasts, we are currently seeing a rise in marketing noisemakers.

They will report on Google Analytics performance, numbers of clicks on links and shares, and other social engagements. What they cannot report is a person reaching out to the company—and that is the purpose of marketing today. While I realize this can be debated, the business case for marketing noise has yet to be made.

The diligent sales focused CEO will continually look at waste elimination within the sales and marketing businesses, and will constantly assess them for improvements through internal or external analyses that can be performed randomly. The larger the sales force your company operates, the more important this becomes.

18 Sales and Marketing Talent Leadership

We have discussed the prerequisites of a sales leader's performance in his or her role. It's important to define those expectations to the point where you as the CEO can check off a list and decide who's on your team. Sales leaders are pivotal to the team delivering results, since sales forces are typically a direct reflection of the sales leader after ninety days. The sales leader at all times communicates the standards and influences the behaviors of the sales team, whether they're applying performance-management cultures, autonomy cultures, or variations of either. If the sales leader lacks skills for today's hardened commercial requirements, then you're exposing your company to risk.

As CEO, you need to have your sales leaders assessed against current best practices, knowledge, and skills in order to evaluate any additional skills they may need. If the sales leaders are receptive to training, you need to invest in their development. Interestingly, however, sales leaders receive the least amount of training and mentoring of any other members of the sales organization, even though their roles are critical to success. These poorly skilled individuals are often promoted for their selling capabilities and customer relationships, and are rarely challenged to understand or deliver the full requirements of their new managerial roles. Those sales leaders who are open to education can be developed into excellent commercial sales leaders, thus becoming outstanding assets to the company.

Those who do not accept education may need to have their talents applied to other areas of the business.

During research SFI conducted in 2009, we found several alarming trends in sales leaders' capabilities. This was at a time when sales leadership was being scrutinized like never before due to the global financial crisis.

Generation 1 (the Most Unskilled of Sales Leaders)

- Customer targeting
- Sales meetings or gatherings on an ad hoc basis
- Individual or team budgets
- Basic compensation plans
- Product sellers usually have little consultative selling capability
- Team reporting is verbal
- Performance is measured on the basis of historical figures

Hiring criteria for team members include industry experience, strong sellers, personal likability, customer connections

Generation 2 (Shows Some Form of Leadership Process)

- Immature territory management strategies
- Immature account management strategies
- Performance reviews are done annually
- Individualized budgets, with under budget performance acceptance
- Sales trainings at irregular intervals
- Individual coaching on an ad hoc basis
- CRM systems seldom taken up within teams
- Product sellers typically use a consultative approach

Hiring criteria for team members include industry experience, strong sellers, personal likability, a strong customer base, attendence of sales trainings, and optional CRM exposure.

Our research found that Generations 1 and 2 are the most populated area of sales, with 78 percent of sales leaders falling into these categories. Within this grouping, 34 percent reported that they would not adopt any changes to their practices. This is alarming, since it means that the pool of potential sales leaders is small, and they will be in high demand.

The talent you need to hire must possess, at minimum, the following primary traits:

- Sales planning

- Human capital planning

- Cost control of sales headcount

- Knowledge management

- Sales cost control

- Risk management—human capital

- Risk management—financial

- High-uptake implementation of CRM system

- Sales compensation and rewards aligned with corporate goals

- Cross-organizational efficiency

- Quarterly performance reviews

- Brand management—human capital

- Analytical/strong follow-through on tasks

- Leadership based on set goals and requirements within team

- Role clarity

- Strong induction and educators

- No individual greater than the business in his or her knowledge

- Lead-tracking systems in place

- Defined selling practices in place

Hiring criteria for team members include suitably degree-qualified people, strong sellers, people who have worked within the structure, consultative selling capability, professional training, territory management capability, sales channel experience (rather than industry experience), ability to learn new products rapidly, and people who use technical resources to their advantage with customers.

These are the sales leaders who will be in high demand in the future; companies need to set these leaders' standards for the future. Once the sales leader has developed the necessary skills for delivering results, the need for genuine performance management of the team becomes pivotal. Performance management ensures that strategy execution is completed and that sales goals are consistently met in an effective and efficient manner. Performance management, in contrast to autonomy-style management, focuses on the performance of the sales organization and the sales team members. Performance management means providing high levels of coaching that assists people in staying on plan and removing any barriers that prevent them from producing.

Sales leaders need to understand performance management content and culture. They also need to know what's expected of them in order to support the overall sales business. Even if they have a great deal of experience, don't assume that they will know what they need to do differently in the future. These are high-organizational-profile hires, and you must apply due diligence when hiring them. The usual hiring practices will not identify them, since they do not understand their new role requirements; as a result, you will be unable to ask them relevant questions in order to ascertain their capabilities. All sales leaders talk about systems and processes, profit, and other popular statements and words of leadership during interviews. Few implement them upon commencement in their new jobs, however, since doing so would put them in the spotlight. You need to hire a person who's accustomed to operating under the spotlight and has the talent to deliver—: a person who embraces change and improvements, both for him- or herself and for the team.

If you have long-standing sales leaders in your company, then you need to consider their current contributions to the company—not yesterday or in years gone by, but today. If they do not embrace fresh thinking and contemporary business practices, then their longevity is limited within the sales leadership role. If they do not want to be educated, then they will have an even shorter lifespan in that leadership role.

Marketing talent is a little different; marketers are more likely to adopt change since they thrive on being different. They look for the latest and greatest in marketing techniques, software, and go-to-market methodologies. Marketing is complex in terms of talent requirements, as the field now has many aspects, and people have refined their capabilities so that they've become experts in specific areas. Many marketing services are now outsourced on a user-needs basis for this reason. For example, a content marketer will likely not excel at using Google AdWords; these are now two different skills, even though the conversation may be similar.

As other examples, a web designer is not necessarily someone who will excel at creative design in other mediums, and someone who undertakes the formulation of an e-newsletter is not necessarily a person who will adapt to the requirements of marketing automation; the complexities of business strategy will mean that the value from the automation eludes them.

One issue I frequently find in reviews is that because marketing people are passionate about specific areas of marketing, they will often shift their company's business to the areas they're most passionate about and will justify why the business needs to go to those areas. As a result, one area of the marketing function is strong, many others are weak, and some aren't touched at all.

Marketing today is more than ever a finely tuned area of the business that requires the capability to balance and deliver outcomes. The most important marketing talent to hire today are those who understand strategy and know how to manage projects and resources—people who can understand and write strategy and utilize specialist resources to deliver the components within the strategy, as and when required. They have a view of the entire strategy and have not honed their skills in one specific area; they understand that the customers—and not the trends that marketing companies sell—drive how the marketing sector will operate within the company.

An interesting twist on marketing leaders is that they need excellent analytic skills (not common to marketing) in order to ascertain how they can improve campaigns and events for delivering increased sales lead numbers. They need to look at ways of minimizing marketing efforts while maximizing the output; they must be strong on reporting that uses commercial thinking rather than the cultivation of noise.

They must be willing to work closely with sales in order to eliminate leakage between marketing and sales and to deliver high-quality leads to sales.

The talent in any organization defines its success. Talented people in marketing and sales have a very high profile and obvious capability, both to the customers and within the company. The sales focused CEO like you sets the bar high when hiring for these two areas and demands evidence of their talents through their delivery of your strategy. The measurement of sales and marketing plays an integral part in demonstrating their performance.

19 Measuring Sales Force Performance

Many companies have been indoctrinated into believing that the sales force measurements that should be applied include financial reports with gross margins and pipeline reports. These are the two reports that sales leaders are most comfortable with, and they are the bane of any CEO who tries to work with them. For the sake of clarity, the reference to pipeline reports in this book is the same as opportunity pipeline reports or sales funnel reports. They are simply different terms that have been coined by software providers of customer relationship management (CRM) software.

How many times have you received pipeline reports that started to fall apart under even the first layer of scrutiny? Such reports always present numbers that show the outstanding opportunities that are available, but always in the future. Everything looks wonderful at the start of each month, and then the pipeline slowly diminishes to a very low ending number. Most of those opportunities have been moved to the next month, only to suffer the same fate. Pipelines are designed to track new business or larger sales within customers; what they do not do is track forecasted revenue by customer. (I did review a steel company several years ago that had completely customized its CRM to do just that, but the company had also removed the new opportunity measurement, which was quite ironic.)

The immediate fault in every sales pipeline I see is that the stages are poorly mapped.

Several sales training companies offer applications that can plug in to popularized software to create what they believe to be the right process. Again, during a recent review of a sales and marketing organization, we looked at the pipeline. It was tailored by using one of these apps, but it failed to provide an accurate view of the velocity in the pipeline. The terms were too generalized, and the "probability factor" had become a loose weapon in the hands of the sellers. Regrettably, this pipeline is now promoted by a major training company that has marketed its new selling process extensively.

To take a step back, let's look at that probability factor. For those who are not familiar with the term, it is a percentage that is applied to each opportunity as it moves across the different stages. The revenue projections are then calculated based on those percentages—a fool's paradise, if I have ever seen one in business. I often say, "If you are using the probability factor, you are probably going broke." It is the first thing I shut down in any CRM. Why? The probability is a salesperson's subjective view about the likelihood that the deal will close. Salespeople are not stupid, and they will load the percentage up when they're under pressure and back it down again when they're not. They will also hold deals back to avoid scrutiny, which means that you as a CEO will not have a true understanding of where things stand. If the pipeline reports that are presented to you require interpretation, then they are not being done correctly. Measuring sales force performance is complex, which explains why the average sales leader rarely gets openly excited about the thought of the sales force being measured correctly; you can be confident that such leaders are not the instigators of that measurement.

As we have discussed throughout this book, sales is a high-risk area of the business, as is marketing in the new world that business trades in.

Measurements must be implemented that provide rich information on which you can base decisions and thus understand the heartbeat of your sales organization. That level of information is also necessary for effective coaching of team members to improve their performance—another task that is not popular with the average sales leader.

As part of my consulting work, I implement measurements on sales and marketing organizations across many different industries. There is no cookie-cutter approach, since every company is different and has different drivers; the first mistake is to make them all uniform. The drivers in IT companies, for instance, are not the same as those of industrial companies, and medical businesses are not the same as professional service-style businesses. When you look for rich and valuable information, you need to drill deeply into the heart of the company and identify the drivers that will deliver your strategy in your industry.

Those measurements can change from year to year as you change the strategy for dealing with market pressure. As you shift to new markets, new countries, and new structures in sales and marketing, the measurements must shift with you; if they do not, then you are simply not measuring sufficiently to minimize the risk in your business.

Another interesting point about the measurement is that the culture of the company will define how the measurement is received. Companies that are led by arm's-length management will have uprisings against measurements, which means a large proportion of companies that experience issues of varying degrees. While people may nod politely when you first discuss the measurements with them, after six weeks, their real "acceptance" of the measurements will become clear. The information should always be designed to be used for risk management and the coaching of individuals; it is not meant for finding reasons for moving lower performers out of the business.

To assist you in understanding the different measurements that can be used, below are some of the more common points for giving you insights into an individual's performance.

They will provide you with the first layer of information for making a few decisions:

- **Average sale size:** What size sales do the salespeople close? How quickly do they discount sales? How well can they negotiate? Average sale size provides insights into how well salespeople can manage larger sales opportunities, maintain the integrity of pricing, and drive greater value into the sale.

- **Win/loss ratio:** This is typically measured now through CRM, but it is seldom reviewed closely enough. You need to know what percentage of opportunities the salespeople close. How effective are they with the opportunities they uncover, or with leads they're handed? A higher winning percentage suggests that they have an impressive ability to qualify or add substantial value to the sale. High winning percentages mean that fewer leads and opportunities are wasted.

- **Average days in the pipeline:** How long do sales sit in the pipeline? How good are the salespeople in knowing when to stop working a sale and close it? How often do they sit on opportunities that will never come to fruition? Are their pipelines full of dreams (or padding)? Is there a decent ratio between average days in the pipeline and average time to close?

- **Average time to close:** How long does it take salespeople to close a sale from start to finish? Who in your sales force closes sales fastest? Who takes the longest? How do average-time-to-close rates compare with sales goals and overall revenue achievement? If they're out of sync, then revenue achievement can be a problem.

Average time to close includes both wins *and* losses; it is designed to measure the amount of time it takes a salesperson to bring a buyer to the decision.

- **New opportunities per month (NOP):** Who is best at building their pipelines? Which salespeople are focused on new opportunities versus closing existing opportunities? How many new opportunities are your salespeople putting into the pipeline each month? NOP is a critical metric that few pay sufficient attention to. Knowing who is bringing in the opportunities to your company is critical. A salesperson who cannot generate new business is of little value to most companies in today's competitive marketplace.

- **Average monthly pipeline size:** What does the pipeline look like from month to month? Who is good at keeping it consistent in terms of quality, as opposed to those who see big shifts while they close, and then prospect, and then close? This measurement allows you to see who is capable of maintaining a strong pipeline while closing sales and driving revenue; in other words, it lets you see who delivers reliable and predictable revenue to the business.

These examples of several measurement points find patterns of behavior of individual salespeople and how those patterns affect your company's revenue achievement. This behavior is what sales leaders are required to coach and improve. For too many years, companies have relied on (and paid heavily for) what they believe is a star player: a top seller who will bring in the business no matter what. Such people actually become threats to the business, since you cannot afford to lose them. It is poor management for any company when a salesperson becomes greater than the business itself, and you're held "ransom" (intentionally or unintentionally) because you'll lose customers if and when that individual leaves.

Sales encompasses the efforts of *all* individuals, not just a team pooling its results.

With good measurement for individuals, you can see who is contributing and who is not. "Bluebird sale makers" (that is, salespeople who make the sale without much direct effort in securing it) will not be able to bask in the glory of a lucky break that most likely landed in their laps; they will be shown to be poor performers once that first sale is made. Companies today build their sales forces based on average sellers, and work hard to improve those average people. Such people present a lower cost to the company to hire and retain, and are more willing to be performance-managed to deliver the requirements of the strategy. Under these circumstances, the sales leader becomes a coach more than an associate within the team.

When considering behavior, one of the oldest and most ridiculous demands on sales forces I continue to see is the requirement to attend a minimum of ten, twenty, or even forty appointments per week, as a sales leader recently told me. The company was selling a complex product that required good conversations and meetings to close, but the sales force was unable to do so given the immense pressure inherent in their appointment numbers. That man's future as a sales manager of the company was very short!

Should you meet a sales leader who talks of fixed appointment numbers that are more than fifteen per week, you've met someone who does not understand strategy execution. The strategy should define the number of appointments that are required, and will vary from person to person based on each person's sales behavioral patterns and capabilities.

As part of the sales focused CEO management system, measurements must also be put in place that will serve the needs of the salespeople. They must be given a firsthand opportunity to understand the levers they can pull to improve their performance and compare their performances clearly against others' performances.

A salesperson is by nature a competitive person (or should be), and that competitiveness is a great motivator in open reporting across the team. Making this fundamental shift with the sales force will result in executive management having more information to work with; as such, it will be easier for you to identify trends and make quality decisions.

To summarize, the purpose of measurement is to:

- Assist the CEO in removing the risk that poor performance goes under the radar

- Align the sales and marketing business to the strategy, and then monitor that it is still on track

- Provide rich information for making timely and effective decisions

- Improve the overall effectiveness of the sales force through coaching

- Enable salespeople to be drivers of their own self-improvement and performance

Given my years of experience in managing sales forces during business turnarounds, I designed a simple yet effective measurement system. Turning a business around in 90 to 120 days requires deep and rich information that will provide an immediate response to the issues that currently corrode a company's performance. To this end, we developed part of the management system to provide a behavioral tool that would allow salespeople to work out exactly how much effort they need to apply in order to deliver their sales goals, based on their capabilities. This system is monitored and updated weekly, and it gives the salespeople the power to deliver the necessary results. I've called this part of the management system "Sales Focus Money Ball™," since it embodies what the intent is. It has become a popular term among salespeople and management.

From an executive standpoint, this system makes sure you have the right information to ensure that your strategy is delivered.

20 My Sales Force Will Not Play Today's Game

Sales forces are renowned for poor or no reporting. Prying reports from them can be like pulling teeth. They are often required to provide call reports on the people they've visited, and they provide a few checkbox outcomes and statements that are unmeasurable. This relentless chase often sees sales leaders give up and resort to making phone calls in order to acquire updates about the latest news, hoping to generate less paperwork while doing so than they would while generating reports.

Salespeople will by nature wait for a company-generated report before they will cultivate a report themselves. Companies are so used to serving reports to them that this has become an accepted practice. Generally, companies rely on the financial report as the most important report, since the requirement for most companies is "just go out and sell." What was sold does not matter as much as the fact that something was sold. Those days are over. Salespeople have to report, and they have to do it in meaningful ways; that's the new game, and everyone is required to play it.

There is often some alignment in thinking between sports teams and sales teams. Both focus on the motivational side: players are typically in a great mood before they take the field, and the team has great camaraderie, while salespeople often have motivation-based meetings before being sent out into the market to sell.

If you watch any football or baseball game, the announcers constantly refer to each player's performance: who has pitched how many no-hitters and who has stolen the most bases in the postseason. John is best kicking from the left side of the field back across the goals, while Paul is great at across-the-field play. Statistics fly across the television screen, and people debate if a person can or cannot hit a home run or kick a goal.

Sound familiar? Let's look at the term *Money Ball* and see how it came to be so popular in sports. For many years, athletes were seen as gifted talents: they had something that could not be trained, measured, or improved upon. Their athleticism was natural and could not be replicated; elite athletes were to be treasured for their unique skills. This all changed when a man named Billy Beane, general manager of the Oakland Athletics, proved that idea to be completely wrong.

This symbolic image extends to salespeople. Just like athletes, salespeople want to be seen as special people who possess unique talents that cannot be replicated. They have convincingly communicated this virtue for long periods of time. Those same salespeople feel a sense of entitlement in holding to that idealism. While in times past that may well have been the case, that adage is no longer sufficient.

Sports and sales work in the same parallel. Sports statisticians now keep records of every move those elite athletes make. The statistics have become public knowledge, as well as a phenomenon, especially following the 2011 film *Moneyball* (based on Michael Lewis's 2003 book, *Moneyball: The Art of Winning an Unfair Game*), about Beane's efforts to turn his poorly performing players into a winning team. Using statistics to build a team of elite athletes, he selected lower-cost individuals who could contribute the right behaviors and deliver results for the team.

This is the issue that many CEOs now face—they apply that principle to sales forces, using the same philosophy depicted in the book and film.

Management can account for the good and the bad of every move team members make in order to identify their effectiveness and efficiency, thus building highly effective sales forces. Companies now use sales behavioral measurements as contributors to sales force measurement. It is not just a matter of whether you win or lose the sales revenue game; it is how the team plays the game throughout each month, quarter, and year. This measurement can provide you with the vital transparency you need to manage your team effectively.

Sales organizations can benefit tremendously from individual performance statistics, which provide the ability to measure the sales team's "athletes" and thus understand their true effectiveness. This is where they need assistance and guidance to deliver the results and measure the value they contribute to the organization. Needless to say, many CEOs who ask this of their sales leaders may encounter resistance, much like the challenges that Beane met in the film. The old ways are comfortable, even if they no longer deliver results.

For those who take a contemporary view of sales forces and understand the value of behavioral measurement, I developed a methodology (not software based) that provides a process for assisting companies. This is the aforementioned Sales Focus Money Ball. This is an open sales pitch, but I do believe in the value that it brings to companies. If a comparative product is available, then it should certainly be considered. I've used this methodology in more than twenty-five years of consulting work in turning companies around. In recent years, I've found that it resonates with more people now that they've become familiar with how Beane applied the concept with his baseball players.

Sales Focus Money Ball is a planning and management tool designed to assist both executives and salespeople.

For executive management, this includes:

- Planning: Improved sales goal setting that enables higher goals to be set

- Transparency: Having a complete understanding of individual team performance

- Measurement: Having a greater understanding of what is driving the revenue results for your company

- Improved results: Achieving higher revenue across all team members

For salespeople, this includes:

- A valuable planning tool that enables teams to plan how to deliver over sales goal results each month, quarter, and year

- Smarter decisions resulting from using the planning tool, since teams can make more intelligent decisions about their customers, activities, and focus during meetings

- Increased performance, where sales team members are more productive in the critical areas of productivity and effectiveness

- Managing pipelines, which can be validated for more reliable forecasts

- Coaching, in which individual coaching and development needs are identified and easily addressed with situational coaching

Sales Focus Money Ball is not a project; it becomes part of the culture of the company. The most important element of it is the creation of salespeople who think smartly about their performance and drive results. They can ascertain their workload and determine which levers to pull on a weekly basis in order to deliver the required outcomes.

Like all reporting, this does not come easily to sales teams, but their level of engagement will be much higher since they will have a high-value return when they use it. The company will also benefit, of course, as outlined above. Sales Focus Money Ball gets your salespeople to play the game.

 21   Sales Operations Is the New Management Tool

We have discussed reporting, measurement, and metrics in the previous two chapters, and most sensible people are no doubt thinking, *When will we have time to pull all these reports; disseminate, analyze, and discuss the information; and then set out the actions we need to take? Anyone on the senior management team is already starved for time, including the sales leader.*

As sales organizations become more process driven and scientific, sales operations have taken on a new level of importance. Sales operations people are not administration personnel, nor are they members of the inside sales team. They are people who take seats at the executive table and act as the conduits of information for sales force performance and strategy alignment.

A competent sales operations person's primary function is to ensure that there is no leakage in sales analysis, performance, and opportunity management. This individual understands sales behavior in the field, is analytically minded, and is able to prepare reports for the executive and sales leaders to standardized formats in a timely manner. He or she plays a significant role in identifying when the salespeople are not delivering the required activity and conforming to systems—especially pipeline management.

As an extension of their function, sales operations people can ensure that all account plans are being performed, and that the share of the wallet is being maximized with customers. They have the authority to request and follow through on task completion in order to maintain the operational effectiveness of the sales organization.

Sales operations people are forms of analytical sales managers. They bring the sales focused CEO rich information in clean reporting formats in order to support high-quality decision making and reduce the risk of wandering off strategy. Sales operations people provide the details that allow sales leaders to continue having quality conversations with their teams and ensure that the sales business works according to a well-defined sales strategy implementation process.

I've employed many people over the years, and those who've performed the best and added the most value are always those who have accounting backgrounds and exposure to sales. They know how to source, sort, and use the data to create logical reports, and they understand how the data affects sales. They are exceptional with Excel and can create pivot tables from raw data, thus providing the immediate view that executives need. Sales operations people must also be extremely familiar with CRM. For many large, fast-moving consumable goods (FMCG) companies or medical companies, the emphasis in the past has been on sales analysis, due to the enormous number of stock lines such companies have. Sales analysis is a subset of the sales operations role, and it does not represent the full extent of what such people do.

Each company is different, but this overview provides insight into their value to you and the company. The reports should be condensed to one page for sales and marketing that can be drilled down into at the state and individual level. Sales operations people should be responsible for reviewing and reporting on the following:

- **Marketing reports of lead-generation quality and outcome:** These reports directly contribute to the alignment of sales and marketing and allow for determining whether value is generated in leads that will support the sales effort. This alignment includes considerable cost reductions if people remain focused on the reporting process. This should be a one-page report that is insightful and alerts exceptions.

- **Pipeline validation:** Pipelines are complex, and are not just a matter of forecast revenue. Reports should include information about deal times, stalled opportunities, any changes that are made to the pipeline, and any other behavioral issues that will negatively affect the quality of the report. Taking a 360-degree view of the information ensures accurate reporting, and makes sure there will be no slippage of opportunities.

- **Pricing variation reports:** These reports allow for understanding which products and customers are putting the most downward pressure on margins.

- **Account behavior and plan behavior:** Account plans are written much like minor strategies—plans of what can be achieved with accounts, or of those plans that are being targeted. An unmeasured plan becomes just another time-wasting exercise—a great idea that is lost in day-to-day trading.

- **Tender knowledge acquisition and review of plans**: For companies that use tendering as part of their sales processes and for contracts that require renewals (an important factor), this is a primary or secondary line of defense in ensuring the performance of the contracts, and making sure that full value is realized on existing contracts. Such plans also ensure the timely preparation of upcoming tenders.

- **Sales behavior:** Sales Focus Money Ball reviews the adherence to (and quality of) data that populates the management reporting, which is the heartbeat of the sales force.

- **Sales plan implementation and progress:** When performing these steps, the strategy is set, the sales plan is designed, and sales operations monitors that all the contributors occur in a timely manner.

- **Adherence to policy and process:** Including sales proposals/contracts is an important function in the company. If you rely on sales leaders to manage this, the slippage soon becomes a lost requirement, and there is no monitoring or adherence.

- **CRM adherence, and, in particular, pipeline task completion and diary management**: In many companies, CRM has become the centerpoint of sales information about customers. Salespeople do not engage voluntarily, which means that those who get a little behind or off track must be continually monitored. Conducting simple reporting and confirmation through cross-referenced reviews ensures that the CRM has quality information and is not just another "legacy" item with low adoption rates.

- **Compensation and reward program eligibility and achievement:** This is an important part of the process for midsize companies that do not have a dedicated compensation manager for rewards and incentives. (Note that this only applies if the program is added to employees' salary packages.)

From reading the lists of information that the sales operations people give you, you can see a trend of compliance and gain various insights into performance.

This process means looking at data from different directions in order to create useful reporting that you can then base important decisions on; it also means providing useful reporting to create conversations between marketing and sales leaders, and between sales leaders and their people for coaching. These reports provide the tools that sales leaders need to perform their jobs, manage their sales teams, and deliver planned results.

I cannot imagine a company not having a sales operations person in place at the executive table for meeting today's business requirements. These people provide invaluable support to the sales focused CEO.

22 Removing the Chasm between Marketing and Sales

The American Marketing Association most recently defined *marketing* as "the activity, set of institutions, and processes for creating, communicating, delivering, and exchanging offerings that have value for customers, clients, partners, and society at large." The techniques used in marketing include choosing target markets through market analysis and market segmentation, as well as understanding methods of influence on customer behavior. The definition of *sales* is "the act of selling something through the exchange of goods, services, or property for money."

The marketing definition overlaps with the sales definition through the word *exchange*. While both have the same intent, sales and marketing have in the past struggled to work well together, at great expense to their companies. In fact, many sales and marketing teams barely speak to each other—never mind working together. Alignment between marketing and sales involves many things: a sound understanding of the company strategy; shared goals, with common milestones and metrics; streamlined business processes; and smart technology investments that provide a single view of the customer experience for both marketing and sales.

First and foremost, however, alignment means one thing: communication.

If sales and marketing cannot learn how to work together as a single team, speak the same language, exchange information freely, and have a clear understanding of what a lead is, then all the planning and measurement in the world will not make a difference. They must be one united team. The benefits of alignment are clear: according to a 2011 Aberdeen Group study, highly aligned organizations achieved an average of 32 percent year-over-year revenue growth, while their less-aligned competitors saw a 7 percent decrease in revenue. According to another study (from Forrester), a mere 8 percent of companies say that their sales and marketing units are tightly aligned.

Many different views exist about marketing's contribution to a company: some focus on branding, and some on awareness to new audiences, while others focus on web presence or sales leads.

Branding is an area that can generate expenses with little to no return; this is a visual format that satisfies people, since the company's presence can be seen in many different mediums. The Internet now plays an important role in how potential customers find companies, and the rise of Google has influenced many marketing-related tasks. Branding can be a resource-burning, nonreturn function if it is not handled by professionals. With so many varying views, it's easy to understand why marketing has become so confused in its purpose. I would clarify the function of marketing to an even narrower intent: *the purpose of marketing is at all times to build the brand and presence of the company in the market, with the intent and purpose of generating quality leads for the sales force.*

The market has changed, and today it is imperative that marketing and sales be aligned and contribute to the execution of the company strategy. Never before has such emphasis been placed on marketing's ability to generate quality leads.

With traditional practices such as cold calling no longer a reliable lead-generation method, marketing organizations must be engaged in demand generation, thus taking up the function that sales organizations previously performed.

Today, new buyers are entering the sales process much later, and marketing must capture those buyers and engage them during the early stages of the potential buyers' exploration. The Internet has changed how customers buy: most will only engage with sales once they have reached the point of final selection. Influencing buyers has become more difficult, since they operate stealthily for most of the process. Once buyers appear, sales must seamlessly handle them through to closure, which requires careful management.

With this new emphasis on marketing's involvement in lead-demand generation, the problem for many marketing teams is that they're working on a moving target: sales. The sales business often operates within an autonomous managerial style, where opinions and demands are based on subjective views of what is needed to support sales. Each salesperson operates independently, and marketing attempts to connect with those moving targets. There is an insatiable, never-ending demand for leads, which are then just left to go stale.

Another challenge I often observe is that the sales organization focuses on different products and services than what the marketing organization is focused on, thus leaving a chasm where potential customers can slip through. Neither is aligned with the strategy; they're both caught up in their own worlds because they don't communicate. During reviews, you hear the usual feedback that the sales organization doesn't hear about campaigns until they've already been released, and that the reports' contents are not relevant or correct.

The marketing organization, meanwhile, complains that all of its efforts are falling on lazy salespeople who fail to follow up on the leads they've been provided with. The lack of communication is glaringly obvious in these cases, as is the lack of planning; this creates a high cost of marketing and sales for the business, because the two units are not focused on strategy execution.

Undoubtedly for many companies, although they may have strategies in place, they do not have sales plans in place; that situation dislocates the marketing organization's ability to define the actions that are required to generate sufficient leads to support the sales organization's activities. The lack of planning also inhibits the ability to produce leads within defined markets that will support strategy.

For companies that focus their efforts on customer protection, with little to no new customer activity, the function of marketing slips to becoming a branding exercise, and is often the more company-ego-driven type than the value-driven type. Companies spend money on showing up at the right trade events and sponsoring the right events, and some even get to the point of having lavish sales tools that are rarely used.

Companies that are in business today need new customers. The customer attrition rate is affected by market changes and demands that are beyond anyone's control; as a consequence, we all must have plans in place for the ongoing development of new customers at a rate that exceeds the attrition rate. This requirement for lead generation affects each and every company, and requires the sales and marketing organizations to be attuned to each other.

As the start to achieving alignment between marketing and sales, the marketing organization must have a sales plan that articulates its requirements related to lead generation and the opening of new markets, as well as the timely implementation of those campaigns.

From there, a twelve-month marketing plan can be developed that outlines all of the marketing and communications activities. A concise strategy must be developed that clearly defines how the objectives will be achieved, and includes a communications plan that is backed by measurable goals and objectives. Without such a plan, marketing is operating on its own and can end up delivering mixed messages to customers and prospects, which will have a direct impact on the organization's ability to generate high-quality leads. In addition, without sufficient planning, the overall effectiveness of the marketing effort will be reduced significantly. When your company has strategically aligned communications, in contrast, it leverages them and consistently presents a unified message to your customers and prospects. This effectively increases lead-generation results and people's propensity to spend more.

Marketing and sales need to be speaking the same language. One area where there is often conflict is in buyer profiles. Without the plan as a central focus point, each business unit will most likely have a different view of the ideal prospects for the business—and they may not even know it. Having the plan in place assists in solving this problem. Your sales and marketing leaders need to discuss and agree upon prospect profiles and consider where they overlap and where they do not. They need to review the current profiles against which profiles will be needed in the future to support the company's strategy. They must both work to build a single, mutually acceptable set of prospect profiles. In the process, you'll build an important bridge between your sales and marketing teams that will facilitate better communication and cooperation, and will go a long way toward resolving the entrenched conflict.

The next frontier that causes animosity between marketing and sales is confusion over what the term *lead* means to the two organizations.

I make the definition very clear: *a lead is a person who has reached out to the company and has demonstrated an interest in a product or service, or it is someone who is seeking a resolution to his or her problem.* The key point here is that *the person reached out.* Reaching out means asking a question and engaging in discussion, or inviting someone for a discussion. Reaching out does *not* mean getting the name and address of a person who has received marketing content during outbound campaigns that were undertaken by marketing; these are simply contacts who are nurtured, educated, and engaged, and who will require considerable sales effort to be moved into a sales process, since the conversations often happen too early in the buyer process. This duplicates the cost by having both sales and marketing involved too early in the process.

Where the lead is clearly defined, the conversion rate is high, and the potential spending of the buyer is higher. It is important to note that this will shorten the sales cycle and will support improved sales performance.

The next area for review is content. Many marketing and sales organizations currently have different conversations with customers and potential customers. Many marketers still use features and benefits as their primary means of sending messages, whereas sales has moved on to applications and solutions. For the buyer to have a seamless experience, the messages that are sent must be in sync. Marketing and sales should conduct a review in which the two organizations discuss marketing materials, as well as how to best communicate the intent of the marketing messages. Both must agree that the marketing pieces will communicate the right message and give the buyer the correct information, thus creating quality leads. Most important, the messages must be pitched to the right profile of customer and not be generalized across *all* customers.

If you have developed a clear plan and have defined the leads that are required, and if there is common agreement between the content message and what a lead is, then the next area of alignment is how those leads are managed. The process of handing off leads from marketing to sales is critical to both sides. This is the point where the marketing team proves its value, and the sales team gets the opportunity to close deals. The marketing organization should maintain a register of leads, and the sales organization should document sales outcomes. Depending on the CRM system that is used in your business, this can be an automated process, or it may require manual management. What you do not want is for leads to vanish into a black hole.

The two organizations should have an agreed-upon timeline of when leads will be followed up on, and feedback on the outcome of that initial conversation should be immediately sent to marketing. This communication is vital for knowing if the lead should stay with marketing or if it should be moved over to sales. Both sides of the lead-management process must have accountability. An often-overlooked concern is that when leads are handed over, the marketing team provides little information. The marketers provide information about the particulars of the lead, not about the customer experience with the company. I often find marketing and sales working in separate software environments, which creates a disconnect in the transfer of information about the customer experience.

CRMs should be a "single window" into the customer experience with both marketing and sales. Some platforms can achieve this, with integrated applications that support marketing efforts. There must be one database that everyone works to, where either marketing or sales can click on any given person or record and view the entire customer experience.

This can greatly enhance the sales conversation and can increase the conversion of leads, because people in both marketing and sales can now view the subject matter that the prospect has clicked on, received, or expressed interest in over a given time period. Marketing automation technology can assist companies in accomplishing this goal by giving their sales and marketing teams greater visibility in terms of the way in which prospects and leads move through the marketing, and then sales, pipelines.

Alignment is a lifetime process for any company; it is not a short-term project. A sales focused CEO like you should receive reports that demonstrate the performance of the strategy by way of generating the right velocity in the marketing funnel, the right customer profiles, high-quality leads, and good closing ratios by sales. The key is to ensure continual improvement, with an emphasis on planning, communication, and performance. When these factors are connected in your company, you achieve alignment between sales and marketing; the results will go directly to revenue and the bottom line.

23 Bringing It All Together

The sales focused CEO is one who operates with good strategy and execution plans that are detailed in both the marketing and sales business organizations. There are clearly defined tasks for each and every person, measurement, and transparency, and of course there is accountability. The CEO looks deeply into the business and ensures that all of the actions are taken through one-page reports of the right business drivers. The CEO's reliance on financial reports is balanced with behavioral reporting.

As a sales focused CEO, you place new demands on those who are in marketing and sales; you manage their performance rather than abdicating it to autonomy-style operators. As CEO, you are focused on the business of marketing and sales, since these two areas alone can make or break the execution of your strategy and will define the experience of the year ahead for the entire company. Quite often, CEOs deem underperforming marketing and sales teams to be unacceptable, although having the tools and transparency to minimize the occurrence of such underperformance can assist.

Like anything, new initiatives, new thinking, and contemporary practices require change. Making the shift to becoming a sales focused CEO requires good planning and execution of a well-managed project.

It is very easy to be pulled left and right and away from the core focus of what is required while people deal with the impact of the change in the business and in their roles. The degree of change depends on the current operating disciplines of the business and the culture of the people. One thing you must never do is underestimate the impact of change. Change is difficult for any company, and most of all for a CEO. You are the person who is standing up, exposed from every angle, as people watch, listen, and follow your leadership. Your personal ability to cope with change will have a direct impact on the experience of the company. The speed of change you can cope with will also lead the company in the rate of adoption it experiences.

As discussed earlier in this book, while many people become elated at the thought of leading change, very few have the capability to bring change to fruition. Change is a process that must be completed in a finite time frame. You do not want your enterprise to be forever engaged in change, or else the teams will become battle weary and inevitably produce lower results.

Change is where the business is undergoing major shifts in how it operates. Improvements are continual small adjustments being made to keep the business competitive.

Change that is delivered too slowly dissolves into the achievement of negligible differences. I often refer to this situation as one where people adapt to the things that are easy and nice to do and leave the difficult-to-do things (which *do* make a difference) on the shelf. Change that is implemented too quickly, and by inexperienced people, has a similar effect. The changes are performed at a moment in time and are not embedded deeply enough in the company culture to make any real difference. They become flashes in time rather than actual change.

I worked with a CEO several years ago who needed to implement change since his business was in its third year of a plateau.

His greatest challenge was that he was used to delegating tasks in a manner whereby people were continually focused on different projects before the previous ones had been completed. Little reporting was done outside of verbal meetings where people confirmed that all was well. I consider this type of delegation to be abdication, due to the lack of quality reporting and quantifiable measures. He was influenced by long-standing employees who were excellent at championing their own causes. One of those employees, in particular, was a very divisive and self-centered individual. He had learned to sit patiently through the initial stages of a project and would then appear to accept the change, with no real intention of engaging—a true passive-aggressive type. When the opportunity was right, he would derail the elements of the change that were most likely to affect him. I would suggest that this one person, above any other contributor, was the cause of the plateau in the business. The CEO had to shift from his original practice of abdication and the use of a relaxed communication style, since they'd become barriers to progress for the company. After much counseling and discussion, and under enormous financial pressure, the change started to occur.

Change requires confidence that you're making good decisions. The key to change for any CEO is to ensure that there is good reporting and that you can have difficult conversations with people when required. You need to appreciate that you're not working on a project; you're creating a new way of doing business that will endure for a much longer period of time than any single project. Projects are only about the implementation of the elements that are required, while the company's culture is where sustainability will be generated.

Many change efforts or projects fall by the wayside as people become focused on different projects and tasks throughout the year. The CEO must keep the focus on the reporting and on discussions of the findings in the reports.

The reports need to be relevant, and any decisions that are made based on those reports must be relevant and shift the business forward. They cannot be reports that become just more seldom-opened folders shared on the drive somewhere. As CEO, your feedback on the reports is as important as those who did the work that you now see in the report.

A well-managed project requires excellent communication, clear definitions of measurement, consistent reviews of performance, and concise mentions of the changes that will be delivered. Everyone involved must be accountable, including the CEO. Again, change within sales and marketing is not a task that can be delegated. If you're not active in the review processes throughout the year, the changes will not happen.

As documented by the aforementioned lean turnaround expert Art Byrne, only 5 to 7 percent of change initiatives succeed when the CEO is *not* active in the process. As CEO, you need to invest your time and energy in the process. Fundamentally, you will need to take several important steps:

- Change how the company thinks about and manages marketing and sales.

- Change how the company completes sales strategy and implementation plans.

- Install a performance management culture where people are measured and rewarded for delivering all of the requirements of their roles.

- Restructure the sales organization to be more aligned with the business requirements, and balanced through the right behaviors and capability of salespeople.

- Increase the new business capability of the business in order to secure larger clients more regularly.

- Improve account and business behavior analyses to make more informed, timely decisions.

- Install lead-generation marketing disciplines that are both measurable and accountable.

Successfully leading a business through change requires having the complete support and engagement of the CEO and directors. You must continually send a clear message to the team that you're dedicated to the outcomes of the change and are operating the business in the new structure and culture. When you change how you prioritize sales and marketing in the business through a more structured and planned approach, those results will be realized.

Successful transformations occur where the changes to the systems and business practices are prepared and then introduced to the team as a complete package. When the changes are implemented on a rolling basis, it creates more strain on the business and reduces the credibility of the transformation. The marketing would be a visual change that typically inspires people that the company is clarifying its message to the market, which in turn clarifies the message internally. The sales systems are readily accepted as part of the transformation.

Another key point is that the last thing a company wants to see is that you're easy on your sales and marketing management and hard on the people who report all the way up the chain. The primary responsibility should be with the sales management and marketing management. You need to set the tone and the pace, and make sure that your company operates as a performance-based culture if you're really serious about results. You have to ask tough questions all the time about business performance and hold everyone accountable for their performance.

As the CEO, you should be available to the people who report directly to you on a daily basis so that any problems can be addressed as they occur. You have to respond by staying on plan and on message at all times. You cannot achieve change through casual meetings that have no structure. The change will occur through the constant correction of minor behaviors on a daily or weekly basis, rather than by leaving time for the wrong habits to take hold.

As CEO, you must be comfortable making other people uncomfortable if you want to achieve big change. You need to change the business philosophy to its core in order to effect change that will deliver the results you want. The entire business must be dedicated to change, and not just the sales and/or marketing organization. The change process must take no longer than twelve months to fully complete; ideally, the wholesale changes should be completed within six months of that time frame, and the balance of the time should be used for stabilization.

The question for CEOs and directors is: How focused and strong will you be through the change process? For some companies, the personal confrontation with change is difficult, particularly when the business requirements are not part of your natural behavior in the CEO role. You will not achieve change through collaborative consensus with the team, nor in forming friendships with those involved. The business must set the requirements that will make it successful; people will either engage with you on the journey or they will move on.

Sales Focus International can assist you through the business improvement processes of marketing and sales and, most important, assist you through the leadership change process. We regularly work with CEOs to ensure that the company effects change in a timely and undisruptive manner. We remove the usual trial-and-error phase that is often associated with internally led change.

The most difficult part of this change is the restructuring, culture, and relentless focus on performance management until the change becomes the new way of doing business.

The sales focused CEO is the person who is most capable of delivering greater revenue, profits, and value to the business. When you as CEO are focused on marketing and sales, you will create a highly competitive company that is capable of growth—well above your counterparts in other companies.

Case Studies

Each of the case studies in this section has been put together to provide readers with an insight into the experiences of other companies. We have selected a group of four studies that most closely describe situations that are commonly experienced by many CEOs. We have not focused solely on successful companies, but rather on a combination of both successful and unsuccessful ones. These examples provide a very strong learning process for readers. We have provided two excellent success stories that we feel provide excellent examples of what it takes to become a sales focused CEO.

From this cross section, you will be able to gain invaluable insight into what is—and what is not—required of you if you're to develop your company successfully.

For those CEOs who are looking to transform your companies by using contemporary and fresh thinking about sales and marketing, these case studies provide insights into the different challenges you might face and that you may be unwittingly pulled into by resistant management. Upon reading these studies, you will be amazed by how logic flies out the window in the face of adversity; and how some businesses literally trade into failure because of their inability, and unwillingness, to follow a logical and well-considered process.

Case Study 1:
Is That Your Legacy?

Company	Name withheld
Industry	Manufacturing
Structure	National company in Australia, division of a multinational firm
Number of managers	Five sales leaders and one marketing leader
CEO	Accounting background with strategic capability
Number of personnel	120
Turnover	$45,000,000 per annum

Profile

The company is a well-known corporation in its industry, with a solid reputation for quality product manufacturing and supply. It has been in the Australian marketplace for thirty-plus years and has had the same ownership during that period of time. The CEO is a director of the Australian branch of the company and has held the position for more than ten years.

The company's focus is on product quality and service, and it believes that salespeople are service representatives more than sellers. With recent competition increasing and a price war breaking out in the market, the company has been challenged to meet its minimum product sales requirements, and its margins are under pressure.

The incumbent sales leader has held the position for more than ten years and has been with the business for more than twenty-five years.

Culture

At the time of our review, the company culture was focused on staff stability and the longevity of the staff's relationships with customers in the sales field. The decision-making process was slow, and any actions that had to be taken were also slow to implement (if they were implemented at all). The company had a collaborative management regime, and people from different areas of the business were involved in all organizational decisions. Each business manager supported the nonperformance of other managers since they wanted to maintain the status quo. The executives were highly paid, well above market levels. The CEO enjoyed a facilitator role, believing that the teams were operating with the best interests of the company at heart.

There was little to no accountability across the sales and marketing force; individuals had developed their positions to be greater than the business itself by making themselves conduits for information and decisions. The business was cumbersome and lacked vitality. The company operated with systems that were some eight to ten years behind current business practices. Those systems supported the company in the culture it operated.

Objective

The CEO had developed an excellent strategy several years prior to our review that would have improved the company's current position had the sales leader implemented the requirements. The CEO was now under pressure to change, and he required accountability for the sales team, and to have transparency in their performance and business drivers. He was loyal to the incumbent sales leader and was looking to develop him in the role and to deliver the new requirements.

Issues

We found when reviewing the strategy that it was sound and made good business sense. It required diversification of a few product lines that would expand the markets that were available to the company at the time. The strategy would have provided a good mix between locally manufactured and imported products. The strategy supported having the ability to retain good margins and increase market share without resorting to price to buy the market. The strategy required exploration of new product verticals to source products that were complementary to the company's market. The strategy was developed several years prior to our review, and if implemented would have stopped the company from getting pulled so deeply into the price pressure of the market that it was currently experiencing.

We found when reviewing the business that it was laboring under its culture, with a number of highly paid executives who lacked the skills and expertise to perform the functions to which they had been promoted. Too much emphasis was placed on industry knowledge and the networking of contacts, and too little on the capability to perform functions. I made an immediate recommendation to immediately terminate one of the executives (the commercial manager), as he lacked the skills and attitude required for any business improvement to be achieved. He dominated others in meetings and was a block to the business moving forward.

There were no strategy implementation plans nor any formal reporting disciplines on performance outside of a very complex financial report that was focused on margins.

The sales leader's background was operational; he had no experience or knowledge of sales force requirements and behaviors. His conversation was focused on price and margins, which was in line with the reporting that was being generated. He was a very low-energy person who spoke in a monotone, which made it personally difficult to remain engaged in conversation with him.

The sales force was composed of good, honest, hardworking people who were attempting to do the right thing by the company. They were battle-scarred from the pressure and needed some new light shone on how they could perform their roles more easily. When we interviewed each of the state sales managers, they were competent but reflected the sales forces challenges. One sales manager had succumbed to the pressure and was quite a depressing fellow to speak with. He had no solutions for any problems. He was lost to the point that we also recommended him for removal lest the state office get closed down due to lack of profit generation.

We made recommendations to source a new sales leader who would have more exposure to sales forces; and who would establish structure, process, and reporting to drive the business forward and commence immediate implementation of strategy. The CEO's loyalty to his people overrode logic, and th person was given three months to see if he could respond to the changes—a decision that in hindsight the CEO will regret for a very long time to come.

Implementation

The process commenced with a meeting of all of the state managers and a review of a number of factors in the business that could assist in identifying the products and customers where the most leverage could be gained in the short to medium term. The managers were positive and put good efforts into the analysis; they set plans for the months ahead. While the CEO and managers were positive, the sales leader was frustrated and uncomfortable with the changes. The CEO was to counsel him through the process; his communication style supported such an approach.

The implementation required the sales leader to take a more dominant leadership role by conducting weekly sales meetings with the other sales leaders. He had spent most of his time hiding behind the now-redundant commercial manager, so the new meeting format was challenging and extremely uncomfortable for him. He avoided the meetings, preferring one-on-one conversations with the state managers; he believed that this was sufficient. The sales meetings took some eight weeks to start with the team. The meetings were bland and set a negative tone, since he focused on the problems the company faced.

The CEO was advised that the sales leader was there for solutions, and he had to focus on providing solutions to lead the team forward. This is a vital part of any sales leader's role.

Even with coaching from the CEO, the sales leader was unable to grasp the requirements and continued on his usual path. In the meantime, the market was getting more and more competitive as the price war escalated, and the company's margins suffered.

Despite the sales leader's lack of engagement, the methodologies were gaining traction with the state sales managers. The sales force was penetrating new accounts, achieving sales of a different product mix, and clearing out old stock lines that had been gathering dust for a very long time. The market was responding to their different discussions, and the previously random good sales were becoming more frequent.

The strategy implementation included some positive moves, and the company was set to turn a corner if its focus remained. It was gaining traction very slowly and needed a good dose of energy into the business. The state sales managers were doing their best and grasped what was required of them. The second manager who had been terminated was replaced with a high-quality individual who had a positive outlook; he made good inroads into turning around a problematic business unit.

The sales leader continued to flounder in the demands of the change and sought shelter behind other employees. The exposure of his nonperformance haunted the CEO, who knew he had made a bad decision in not making the decision earlier. The cost of loyalty had now weighed heavily on the business. In a meeting with the CEO and sales leader, I posed the question in very clear terms to the latter: "Is this the legacy you want to leave in this business?" I suggested he consider whether he really believed that he had the talent required for the role, or if it would be better for the company if he stepped aside and let someone else take over. This was now five months into the process, and he had clearly become the roadblock that was stopping it all from happening.

The market was taking its toll on the business, since the company languished under the pressures while waiting for the sales leader to engage and move forward.

Outcome

The CEO had several conversations with the sales leader and eventually decided that the sales leader would step aside to an operationally based role in the company. The new state sales manager was promoted to national sales leader; he was a manager who embraced the new methodologies and systems associated with Sales Focus Money Ball.

The company immediately responded with a desperately needed sense of energy and focus. The business was back to where it had been during week six of the process; it had lost five months of trading opportunity while supporting one individual during the change. His legacy was that he had stopped the business from growing and achieving change.

The company now implements a strategy whereby the CEO has excellent transparency into the company's behavioral performance; he is confident that his company is taking the necessary actions to support the strategy implementation.

Case Study 2:
Yes, I Am Doing It

Company	Name withheld
Industry	Services
Structure	National company
Number of managers	One sales leader and marketing leader
CEO	Accounting background with strategic capability
Number of personnel	100
Turnover	$35,000,000 per annum

Profile

The company is a highly successful and profitable business that is growing exponentially by the year. It has an outstanding brand name in its specific market and is positioned to take on even greater growth in the years ahead. The company is well managed, with excellent cost control and a good understanding of the company's marketplace.

The company acquired a number of smaller players in the market in recent years, which is a strategy that the company plans to continue. The company had also developed expertise in providing outsourced services to large corporations, which it identified as another growth vertical. This is a very well-organized and managed business that has all the necessary ingredients for achieving significant growth over the next five to ten years.

Culture

The culture of the business at the time of our review was good, and everyone was focused on serving customers and providing excellence in service to those customers. The sales team consisted of long-standing personnel and recent hires with a mix of skills and capabilities in the different industries the company provided services to. The home state was its strongest market; the company was expanding into other states with acquisitions and the hiring of new sales personnel.

The sales leader conducted regular meetings and scrutinized what people were doing and where they were focusing their efforts. Opportunity and financial reports were used for reviewing the company's performance. The company had a solid grasp of forecasting existing customers.

Issues

Upon review of the business strategy and growth requirements, our report identified that a marketing person was necessary to complement the sales organization's activities and to break new ground for them. The salespeople would be required to become 100 percent sales focused and to break away from the customer-service-style approach that had supported them to date. This would be a significant cultural change for them.

The reporting, although extensive, did not focus on the business drivers; it failed to provide sufficient insight into the business that would allow for effective decision making by the CEO. Our review determined that the company was a good business that required greater transparency into the strategy implementation to ensure that the company was hitting its goals in a timely manner.

Implementation

The sales leader, also a director of the company, was charged with the responsibility of implementing the new methodologies and systems. By nature, he was a person who operated on his own, and he enjoyed a good degree of autonomy. Since he had a science background, he would review things thoroughly before doing any implementation; he wanted to fully understand all implications of a change before it was made.

Meetings confirmed that the company was implementing the recommendations, but very little evidence for this came forward. The CEO took the position that if someone advised that the change was happening, then it was happening. This is how the business had operated successfully to date, and he had no reason to doubt that it would not continue this way in the future. The company liked an arm's-length association with consulting advisors; this situation would not change unless it saw that there was a reason to do so.

The company hired a new marketing person who had broad experience in similar technical environments; he was charged with pulling all of the assets together and creating a calendar that would support the sales implementation plan.

A number of e-mails were sent back and forth, querying various elements of the methodology; all of this communication appeared to signify that the change strategy was being worked on. Sales were on the rise and were exceeding the company's forecast numbers, so no flags were raised.

After several months, we applied pressure to view the system and the results. Finally, the system was sent through for review and discussion of the results. When we looked at them, we found that they had been completely changed from what had originally been recommended; we could not follow what had been done. The report showed a bizarre mixture of measurements, to the point of even including a rolling compensation calculator for commissions on weekly sales—typically something that would not sit inside the systems.

The system had been changed to what the sales leader believed was needed; he had aligned it to his former systems and thinking. The results were fundamentally corrupted and focused on the wrong information. The spreadsheet that drove it was complex and disconnected from the information that is part of the Sales Focus Money Ball methodology.

It took several days of review and many conversations to get to the bottom of the problem. The challenges the company faced were that the sales team was already introduced and working on the system, and that the company would lose credibility if it made too many changes. The process was working to some degree, but it was not going to provide what the company needed to deliver sales goals by the end of the year. More transparency and measurement was required.

After much deliberation, a path was set that would eventually get the company back where it needed to be. This made the process more difficult than it had to be, but the hope was that it would ease the concerns of the staff so that they would not become unmotivated or lose their engagement with the process. This was a classic case of making a difficult task out of something that was logical and simple to implement.

The CEO discussed the issue with the primary shareholding director; together, they decided that the CEO would take over managing the sales team. This would ensure that the company was on track with what was required. This would be an interim process; the CEO's executive assistant would aid him in preparing reports and doing all the work that was necessary. He would fundamentally lead the sales meetings each week and would hold necessary conversations one-on-one with the team. The sales leader would remain a business development director, where his capabilities were outstanding.

Within one month of the change, the systems were starting to make sense. The executive assistant was capable of drawing the right information from different systems; he could connect the information in such a way that the strategy was shifting back to the original intent of the Sales Focus Money Ball methodology. The sales meetings became shorter and more focused, and people were becoming aware of the fact that they needed to operate in the market in order to deliver results. They were thinking and making decisions based on quality data and on streamlining and focusing their efforts.

Outcome

The company has become more aware of the contribution that marketing can make to the sales effort, as well as of the need for marketing to be aligned closely to the demands of sales.

With the change in focus of the CEO from delegation to inspection, the business responded immediately under his leadership; the sales team now acts in a smarter way in its plans and decisions.

The CEO is having better conversations with people about sales and marketing performance, and decisions are made according to the company's requirements. The CEO will eventually extract himself from the process and will appoint a new sales leader who will operate within the systems once he or she is settled. The company is set, and will deliver the growth it originally planned based on the momentum it is now achieving.

Case Study 3:
Ticking All the Boxes

Company	Name withheld
Industry	Construction
Structure	National company
Number of managers	State sales leaders across four state offices
CEO	Engineering background
Number of personnel	150
Turnover	$55,000,000 per annum

Profile

The company has been trading for thirty-plus years; it expanded from its original Melbourne operation through a combination of acquisitions and the opening of new offices. It is well known in the construction industry and has a good reputation for quality products. The company is privately owned and funded, and it has been experiencing issues due to the poor performance of all but one state office.

Culture

The company had developed a culture of operating as individual business units based on financial reporting and the mantra that the business reflected the same. There was little to no interaction between the state offices and no sharing of knowledge or customer interactions to expand the business. The three underperforming state offices were very self-focused and sought to divert attention away from their nonperformance. They had a very well-tuned set of excuses that were difficult to break down due to the lack of informative reporting in the business. They provided many excuses about why the business unit could not excel. The manager failed to engage in business thinking, and the CEO was carrying them. They had all been promoted from within, rather than the company hiring quality people externally. The business had hired externally in previous years, which had caused a recent devastation to one business unit's revenue stream, thus causing the company to again look internally when hiring.

Issues

The company was understandably suffering cash-flow issues due to the lack of sales from three of the four state offices. The protracted time that this took had placed the company in a very difficult trading position. The CEO was dealing with many issues on several fronts and was feeling the pressure.

The finance manager was unable to provide any insights through the reports that would have assisted in decision making.

Each state office had a state manager and a sales leader. Each of the state offices operated a manufacturing facility that was overseen by the state manager. When we reviewed the business, we found that there was a lack of strategy, which is often the case in businesses with cash-flow issues. Each of the state offices were selling products that were difficult for customers to acquire elsewhere, and the company was pushed into doing custom work at a high cost to the business. The sales force was protected by the sales leader, rather than being managed. The culture of the sales force was one of being at war with the executives; it was a true "us versus them" culture in the business.

The business was challenged to continue forward, but the CEO had a steely dedication to trading out of the issues. He needed a running partner to work with who could put in the objectivity that was required to pull the business through; I took up that role with him.

Implementation

We conducted a review of the executive from the worst-performing state office, and the sales leader certainly did not survive more than thirty minutes. He had been appointed by the state manager only four months earlier. The sales had not altered at all during that time. When we met him, he told us that he required his salespeople to do forty appointments per week. That is not a typographical error: *forty appointments per week*. People cannot sell at that level of appointments; they are couriers or brochure salespeople at best. The sales leader had no strategy and no reporting, and he believed in autonomous management. He now has a wonderful career somewhere else. The company did not replace him to save revenue, and the state manager is now responsible for running the sales team.

In the next-worst-performing state office, the CEO went in and conducted a similar review of the personnel. The culture was putrid, with people blatantly ignoring directives from the CEO. That business sales leader also now has a wonderful career elsewhere, as does the state manager. The remaining salespeople are now reporting directly to the CEO (as of this writing) as an interim measure.

The system was implemented, and within one week the business was focusing on sales behavior. The teams were then taken through a process of planning and engaging the Sales Focus Money Ball system. Their defiance and shelter as individual business units was taken away, and they were immediately managed as a national sales team. This was a significant cultural change to the business that came with many objections and the usual disturbances of change. The CEO's steely focus kept the company heading in the right direction.

As the systems and rich information started to come through, the business became smarter about how it was selling. The sales team members understood what was required of them and were able to manage their performance. A little of that sales competitiveness sneaked into the culture, as each state office was out to prove that it was better than the others.

The worst-performing state office had a change of staff and hired new salespeople. The younger and more vibrant team, although new to field sales, was energetic and had product knowledge. The old guard could not handle the pace, including the state manager; the newer people relished the new systems and immediately grasped the value of them.

The second-worst-performing state office was fortunate enough to hire a quality leader who was capable of managing sales and operations; this person was a high-energy and engaging leader, and the team responded accordingly.

The culture changed immediately, with one of the "earmarked" (for dismissal) salespeople turning around his results in six weeks.

The sales meetings were held on a specific day each week, and the state managers' meetings followed the next day. The culture was changing each week, and people were becoming more focused on driving growth. The managers were communicating better, and the business was improving. The CEO now sends out a note each week with the sales results; this provides good feedback to everyone, which has been well received. The culture has shifted from an "us versus them" mentality to one of actual teamwork.

The company now has a clear focus on selling products, which has assisted operations in reducing its costs and achieving continuity in production. The company even shifted to tendering for larger opportunities and new product development. This is a remarkable turnaround for any company to achieve in less than twelve months.

Outcome

Through the steely dedication of the CEO, the systems were implemented in a timely and correct manner. The company achieved 30 percent growth month-on-month for six months, to the point of being above sales goals nationally for the first time in several years. The cash-flow issues started to resolve themselves once the business started to generate consistent sales; this was further assisted by sales of the right products.

The CEO has been able to step away from day-to-day management, but he remains connected with the sales activities through the transparency and rich reporting of Sales Focus Money Ball. The business continues to grow and has the ability to scale now, both of which manage the risk of new hires and nonperformance.

Case Study 4:
Corrupting a Great Business

Company	Name withheld
Industry	Information technology
Structure	National company
Number of managers	State sales leaders across three state offices
CEO & directors	Sales and IT backgrounds
Number of personnel	280
Turnover	$85,000,000 per annum

Profile

This is a high-profile company in the information technology (IT) space that achieved many awards for performance during its early years. The client base is the who's who of blue-chip companies in the country. The company was only eight years old when we first met the employees, and it had been rapidly expanding. The directorship team is all young; its members have excelled in building a highly profitable company. The challenge for the directors was that they had grown the business to a certain size and were unable to break through the barrier to the next level of growth. The company had exhausted its own systems and thinking and was looping at the same revenue level each year.

Culture

The company had a high-energy culture, and people had enjoyed their association with one of the most high-profile IT companies in Australia. The company had a blue-chip client base, and the business made sales despite itself. The blue-chip client base continued to use the company's services, since the company was an approved supplier. The company had become a business with the underlying prosperity of having a "no one ever got fired for hiring them" status. It was a safe decision for companies to make. It was a fun place to be, and people enjoyed working there. The CEO (also the director) had a typical likable sales personality; because people enjoyed working with him, he was able to attract good sales talent through his network.

Issues

The company had made money despite itself as it rode a wave of popular services in the IT market, but it had not learned how to make money nor how to scale a company.

The services the company provided had high profit margins, which had afforded it the luxury of making mistakes without them costing the company too dearly. The directors were all focused in different directions; one of them in particular believed that he was an entrepreneur who was going to identify the next big thing in IT. He would then relive the excitement of the first wave the company had ridden.

The leadership team was all hired through its members' networks, and there was a long history of friendship between them. This meant that any difficult conversations were avoided, and there was a sense of attempting to cajole people into performing the tasks that were required. The sales team was autonomous and could be missing in action for days on end without anyone noticing. The team members had larger-than-life personalities and were handsomely paid for their performance, whether it was over or under sales goals.

Implementation

The CEO stepped aside and looked to have someone else lead the sales team so that difficult conversations could be held. The process was to implement all of the requirements and to hand it back in a structured hand-over process so that the sales force could continue what was implemented.

At first, the sales team was not impressed with being made accountable, but it quickly pulled around. One of the larger-than-life salespeople brought some humor to the first meeting when he announced that the only reason he attended was to see what he could do for us. I quickly suggested that it was a meeting about what he would be doing within the new regime, and that certainly did not go down well with him.

The directors were advised that this would only work if everyone was on the same page, and that they needed to endorse everything together.

If they had issues, they were welcome to raise them privately, but presenting a united front was imperative. Two of the three directors were present at every sales meeting and held to the line at every turn. They sent the message clearly to the teams that it was happening and that they needed to be on the bus. The other director—the would-be entrepreneur-cum-marketer—wanted to go his own way. His actions defied what was required, and he placed a clear line of demarcation throughout the process. The CEO counseled him extensively, as did the other director, but it was similar to managing a two-year-old child.

The business systems and methodology were implemented with relentless focus, and the company immediately responded. Sales were rising at a rate that had not been seen in years. The salespeople, although initially suspicious, quickly worked out the benefits to them and applied the changes to their activities. The worst-performing person, a young man who had not made a sale for nine months prior to our arrival, started signing excellent sales and became one of the company's top sellers. His manager had a line to work to and kept the focus; the plan worked.

The larger-than-life salesperson went from signing $2.6 million per annum to well over $5.5 million per annum, as did his close associate in the business. The culture was good, and the CEO started to step back into his role. Sales were flowing in the door, and the company went from being 20 percent behind sales goals to being 25 percent over sales goals. The company had a scalable business that just needed to hold on to the moneymaking line we had set it on.

The CEO continued with the processes, and sales rose rapidly the following year. Two out of the three directors were more than pleased with the change in their business.

Outcome

Given all the success in the company, surplus funds were available to the directors for personal and business wealth. The third director, the would-be entrepreneur-cum-marketer, had come across a newish innovation and was determined to follow that course with the business. He continued down a path that was going to conflict with the current business operation, and the other directors were at their wits' ends to stop him. Upon our review of the service, it showed high resource requirements for low return. Worst of all, it lowered the overall average booked order value by up to 80 percent, which meant that profits would plummet: clearly, this was not a very good commercial decision.

As the directors struggle with the strategic direction of the company, the business has now changed from being a blue-chip, profit-making business to being somewhat of a low-end provider with a very small business image in the market. The blue-chip operation is still running in the background, but the new service has taken over and has the potential to ultimately destroy the company's reputation in the market while reducing overall profitability.

This is a great example of why strategy is imperative in a company—a strategy that is commercially sound, well documented, and implemented while giving careful consideration to the longer-term view of the company.

To connect with the author:

www.adelecrane.com

LinkedIn:
https://au.linkedin.com/in/adelecrane

Twitter:
https://twitter.com/adele_crane

To read more from Adele Crane, subscribe to:

Blog:
http://www.adelecrane.com/category/business-blog/

www.ingramcontent.com/pod-product-compliance
Lightning Source LLC
Chambersburg PA
CBHW051458170526
45166CB00001B/297